o			
o お オ			
ko こ コ	kya きゃ キャ	kyu きゅ キュ	kyo きょ キョ
so そ ソ	sha しゃ シャ	shu しゅ シュ	sho しょ ショ
to と ト	cha ちゃ チャ	chu ちゅ チュ	cho ちょ チョ
no の ノ	nya にゃ ニャ	nyu にゅ ニュ	nyo にょ ニョ
ho ほ ホ	hya ひゃ ヒャ	hyu ひゅ ヒュ	hyo ひょ ヒョ
mo も モ	mya みゃ ミャ	myu みゅ ミュ	myo みょ ミョ
yo よ ヨ			
ro ろ ロ	rya りゃ リャ	ryu りゅ リュ	ryo りょ リョ
wo を ヲ			
go ご ゴ	gya ぎゃ ギャ	gyu ぎゅ ギュ	gyo ぎょ ギョ
zo ぞ ゾ	**j** ja じゃ ジャ	ju じゅ ジュ	jo じょ ジョ
do ど ド			
bo ぼ ボ	bya びゃ ビャ	byu びゅ ビュ	byo びょ ビョ
po ぽ ポ	pya ぴゃ ピャ	pyu ぴゅ ピュ	pyo ぴょ ピョ

Coming to Japan

Simple Japanese Words & Phrases

ask
PUBLISHING

Table of Contents

Part ③ Communication

Part ④ Sites to See / Must-see Sites / Popular Places

Introduction

「日本を訪れる外国人の皆さんに、日本語を気軽に使ってもらいたい！」という思いから、正しい日本語に固執せず、日常生活でよく耳にする「シンプルなホントの日本語」を掲載しています。文法や文字学習など、複雑な項目はひとまず置いておいて、ページを開ければすぐ日本語が使えます。

This book was written for visitors to Japan to help them communicate easily in Japanese. We avoided focusing too much on proper Japanese in favor of presenting the kind of Japanese that is actually used in everyday life. Putting aside more complicated things like grammar or the study of characters, this book is meant to be used as soon as you open it.

▶ **Part 1**

日本人の習慣、日本語に関する基礎知識を紹介します。

This section introduces Japanese customs and fundamental knowledge about the Japanese language.

▶ **Parts 2 & 3**

Part2では、サバイバル場面で役立つことばを、Part 3では日本語で楽しくコミュニケーションするためのことばを紹介しています。

Part 2 introduces phrases and vocabulary needed in places like convenience stores, restaurants and hospitals. Part 3 introduces phrases and vocabulary used for things like self-introductions, social media and dating.

▶ **Part 4**

日本観光に役立つ読み物のページです。

This sections shows how to properly pray at temples, how to enter hot springs and how to read signs that you might need to know at popular tourist attractions.

You can start at any point you like.

Audio
Track number

This mark shows the store clerk's likely
response, which you 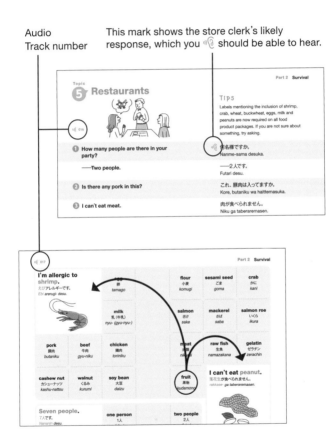 should be able to hear.

Part 2 Survival

Topic
5 Restaurants

Tips

Labels mentioning the inclusion of shrimp,
crab, wheat, buckwheat, eggs, milk and
peanuts are now required on all food
product packages. If you are not sure about
something, try asking.

① How many people are there in your
party?

——Two people.

② Is there any pork in this?

③ I can't eat meat.

何名様ですか。
Nanme-sama desuka.

——2人です。
Futari desu.

これ、豚肉は入ってますか。
Kore, butaniku wa haittemasuka.

肉が食べられません。
Niku ga taberaremasen.

Part 2 Survival

**I'm allergic to
shrimp.**
えびアレルギーです。
Ebi arerugi- desu.

	卵 tamago	flour 小麦 komugi	sesami seed ごま goma	crab かに kani
milk 乳 (牛乳) nyu- (gyu-nyu-)	salmon さけ sake	mackerel さば saba	salmon roe いくら ikura
pork 豚肉 butaniku	beef 牛肉 gyu-niku	chicken 鶏肉 toriniku	meat 肉 niku	raw fish 生魚 namazakana	gelatin ゼラチン zerachin
cashew nut カシューナッツ kashu-nattsu	walnut くるみ kurumi	soy bean 大豆 daizu	fruit 果物 kudamono	**I can't eat peanut.** 落花生が食べられません。 rakkasei- ga taberaremasen.

Seven people.
7人です。
Nananin desu.

one person
1人

two people
2人

Vocabulary words can be
placed where needed in the
phrases.

5

About the Audio

本書の音声はダウンロードサービスとなっています。
This book has downloadable audio.

音声ダウンロードのしかた
How to Download Audio

▶ PCをご利用の方は、下記サイトよりダウンロードできます。

PC users can download the audio from the following link.

https://www.ask-support.com/japanese/

▶ スマートフォン（iPhone, Androidなど）をご利用の方はオーディオ配信サービスよりダウンロードができます。（アプリを事前にダウンロードする必要があります。詳しくは下記サイトをご覧ください。）

Smartphone (iPhone, Android, etc.) users can download the files from the audio distribution service. You will need to download the app beforehand. Please see the site below for details.

https://www.ask-support.com/?p=715

右のQRコードからも
アクセスできます。
The site can also be accessed
using the QR code on the right.

アスクユーザーサポート
Email:support@ask-digital.co.jp

Part 1

About Japanese

Japan, its language and its people

Japanese Characters

Japanese uses three kinds of characters: kanji, hiragana and katakana.

Kanji are originally from China, but those used in modern Japanese are a little different from the kanji used in China. Hiragana were derived from cursive script kanji, while katakana were taken from sections of kanji.

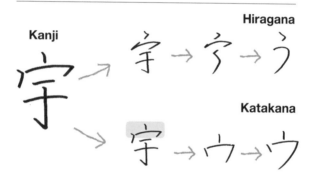

Kanji

Hiragana

Katakana

Unlike English, Japanese is not written with spaces in between words, so using different characters makes it easier to read. However, as there are about 100 hiragana and katakana and thousands of kanji, it takes a great deal of time to memorize all of them.

This book uses the Roman alphabet to show the pronunciation of Japanese words for people who cannot read Japanese characters. These Romanized words are also often used on signs and displays in Japan, but some letters are pronounced a little differently than they are in English. For example, the characters ら, り, る, れ and ろ can be written using Roman alphabet as ra, ri, ru, re and ro. However, the tongue is used differently than for the 'r' sound in English. In Japanese, 'r' represents a sound that is closer to the 'l' sound in English. To avoid confusion, this book uses the most common rules for Japanese Romanization. But, this system does not account for elongated vowels, so hyphens are used to show them more clearly.

Please reference the audio files for any sounds that are difficult to understand.

There is hiragana and katakana on the very first page of this book.

Numbers and Counting on Fingers

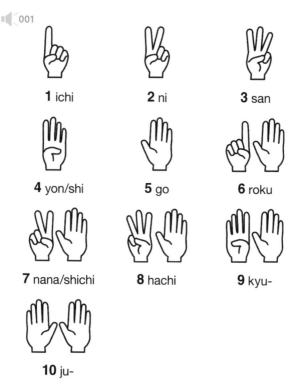

1 ichi   **2** ni   **3** san

4 yon/shi   **5** go   **6** roku

7 nana/shichi   **8** hachi   **9** kyu-

10 ju-

Numbers up to 10 can be shown on one's hands. Numbers above 10 are made by connect different units, for example, 10 [*ju-*] + 1 [*ichi*] = 11 [*ju- ichi*]. Some combinations create variations in pronunciation patters. For example, 3 is *san*, and 100 is *hyaku*, but when combined, 300 becomes *sanbyaku*.

10 ju-	100 hyaku	1,000 sen	10,000 ichi man
20 ni ju-	200 ni hyaku	2,000 ni sen	20,000 ni man
30 san ju-	300 san byaku	3,000 san zen	30,000 san man
40 yon ju-	400 yon hyaku	4,000 yon sen	40,000 yon man
50 go ju-	500 go hyaku	5,000 go sen	50,000 go man
60 roku ju-	600 roppyaku	6,000 roku sen	60,000 roku man
70 nana ju-	700 nana hyaku	7,000 nana sen	70,000 nana man
80 hachi ju-	800 happyaku	8,000 hassen	80,000 hachi man
90 kyu- ju-	900 kyu- hyaku	9,000 kyu- sen	90,000 kyu- man

Phone numbers are read as 01-2345 (zero ichi no ni san yon go) while things like room numbers are read as 201 (ni maru ichi).

Japanese Currency

1円
ichi en

5円
go en

10円
ju- en

50円
goju- en

100円
hyaku en

500円
gohyaku en

1,000円
sen en

2,000円
nisen en

5,000円
gosen en

10,000円
ichiman en

As of 2017, there are currently 10 denominations of currency in Japan. While 2,000-yen bills are in circulation, they are currently in production, so there very rare.

How to Read a Receipt

(After purchasing a drink and bento with a credit card)

Information about the store, such as its address and phone number

24

新宿店

東京都新宿区下宮比町

電話：03-1234-5678　レジ2

2017年5月7日(日)　12:00　責221

領　収　書 — Receipt

ジュース200ML　　　　　　　¥110

お弁当　　　　　　　　　　　¥481

Total — 合計　　　　　　　　　　¥591

（内消費税等　　　　　　　（¥43） — The consumption tax for ¥591, which is 8% as of 2017

クレジット支払　　　　　　¥591

お買いもの明細は上記のとおりです。
商品価格には消費税等を含みます。

This is a credit card note for the customer. In Japan, only one receipt is given, even when paying by credit card — クレジット売上票

会社　　　　　　　　　　　　　　VISA
ご利用日　　　　　　　　2017年5月7日
会員番号　　　　　　　　＊＊＊＊＊1234
支払い方法1回　　　　承認番号123456
金額　　　　　　　　　　　　　¥591
伝票番号　　　　123-456-789-0000

Unit

1. Weights and measures

1 inch = **2.54** cm	**0.393701** inch = **1** cm
1 feet = **0.3048** m	**3.28084** feet = **1** m
1 oz = **28.3495**g	**0.035274** oz = **1** g
1 lb = **0.453592** kg	**2.20462** lb = **1** kg

2. Sizes

Clothes			Shoes		
International	Japan		U.S.	Europe	Japan
XS **(36)**	SS	**(5)**	4.5	35.5	22
S **(38)**	S	**(7)**	5.5	36.5	23
M **(40)**	M	**(9)**	6.5	37.5	24
L **(42)**	L	**(11-13)**	7.5	38.5	25
XL **(44)**	LL	**(15-19)**	8	39	25.5
XXL **(46)**	3L	**(21-23)**	8	41	26
	4L	**(25-27)**	9	42	27
			10	43	28
			11	46	29

3. Temperature

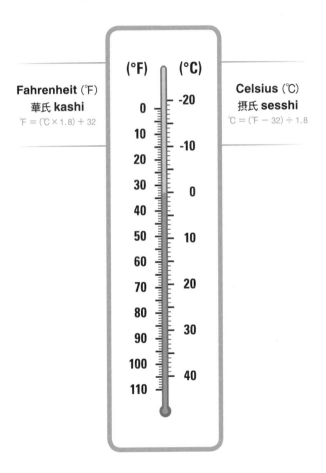

Fahrenheit (℉)
華氏 **kashi**
℉ = (℃ × 1.8) + 32

Celsius (℃)
摂氏 **sesshi**
℃ = (℉ − 32) ÷ 1.8

(°F)	(°C)
0	-20
10	
20	-10
30	
40	0
50	10
60	
70	20
80	
90	30
100	
110	40

Time

～時 ji (~ o'clock)

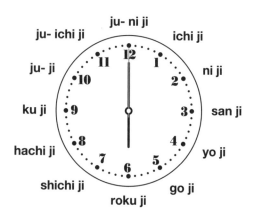

～分 fun (~ minutes)

1	ippun	20	nijuppun
2	ni fun	30	sanjuppun
3	san fun	40	yonjuppun
4	yon fun	50	gojuppun
5	go fun		
6	roppun		
7	nana fun		
8	happun	5時30分 = 5時半	
9	kyu- fun	(**goji** han)	
10	juppun		

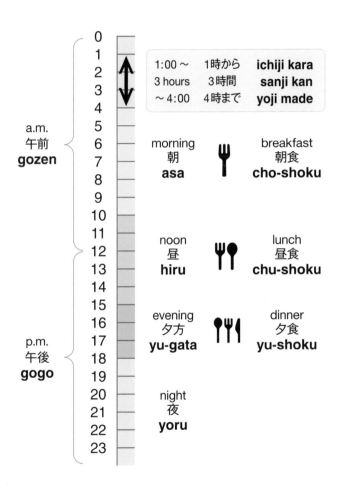

0	
1	
2	1:00 ~ 1時から **ichiji kara**
3	3 hours 3時間 **sanji kan**
4	~ 4:00 4時まで **yoji made**

a.m.
午前
gozen

morning
朝
asa

breakfast
朝食
cho-shoku

noon
昼
hiru

lunch
昼食
chu-shoku

p.m.
午後
gogo

evening
夕方
yu-gata

dinner
夕食
yu-shoku

night
夜
yoru

Calendar

5月

MON 月曜日 getsu yo-bi	TUE 火曜日 ka yo-bi	WED 水曜日 sui yo-bi	THU 木曜日 moku yo-bi
1 tsuitachi	2 futsuka	3 mikka	4 yokka
8 yo-ka	9 kokonoka	10 to-ka	11 ju-ichi nichi
15 ju-go nichi	16 ju-roku nichi	17 ju-nana nichi	18 ju-hachi nichi
22 niju- ni nichi	23 niju- san nichi	24 niju- yokka	25 niju- go nichi
29 niju- ku nichi	30 sanju- nichi	31 sanju- ichi nichi	1

Jan. 1月 ichi gatsu	Feb. 2月 ni gatsu	Mar. 3月 san gatsu	Apr. 4月 shi gatsu
May 5月 go gatsu	Jun. 6月 roku gatsu	Jul. 7月 shichi gatsu	Aug. 8月 hachi gatsu
Sep. 9月 ku gatsu	Oct. 10月 ju- gatsu	Nov. 11月 ju-ichi gatsu	Dec. 12月 ju-ni gatsu

🔊 004

FRI 金曜日 **kin yo-bi**	SAT 土曜日 **do yo-bi**	SUN 日曜日 **nichi yo-bi**
5 itsuka	6 muika	7 nanoka
12 **ju-ni nichi**	13 **ju-san nichi**	14 ju-yokka
19 **ju-ku nichi**	20 hatsuka	21 **niju-ichi nichi**
26 **niju- roku nichi**	27 **niju- nana nichi**	28 **niju- hachi nichi**
2	3	4

2017年5月26日
nisen ju-nana nen / go gatsu / niju-roku nichi

About Japan

Area: **378,000 ㎢**
Population: **126,830,000** (as of 2017)
Language: **Japanese**
Capital: **Tokyo**
National flower: **Cherry blossoms**

🔊 005

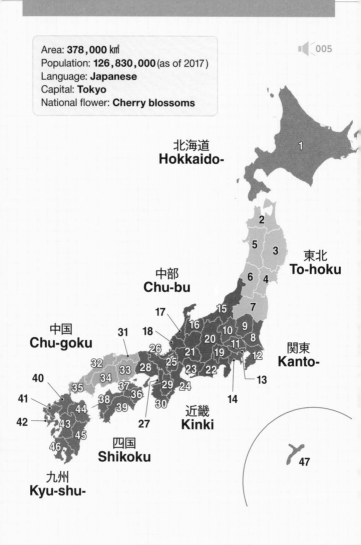

北海道
Hokkaido-

東北
To-hoku

中部
Chu-bu

中国
Chu-goku

関東
Kanto-

近畿
Kinki

四国
Shikoku

九州
Kyu-shu-

47 Prefectures

		16	富山 **Toyama**	32	島根 **Shimane**
1	北海道 **Hokkaido-**	17	石川 **Ishikawa**	33	岡山 **Okayama**
2	青森 **Aomori**	18	福井 **Fukui**	34	広島 **Hiroshima**
3	岩手 **Iwate**	19	山梨 **Yamanashi**	35	山口 **Yamaguchi**
4	宮城 **Miyagi**	20	長野 **Nagano**	36	徳島 **Tokushima**
5	秋田 **Akita**	21	岐阜 **Gifu**	37	香川 **Kagawa**
6	山形 **Yamagata**	22	静岡 **Shizuoka**	38	愛媛 **Ehime**
7	福島 **Fukushima**	23	愛知 **Aichi**	39	高知 **Ko-chi**
8	茨城 **Ibaraki**	24	三重 **Mie**	40	福岡 **Fukuoka**
9	栃木 **Tochigi**	25	滋賀 **Shiga**	41	佐賀 **Saga**
10	群馬 **Gunma**	26	京都 **Kyo-to**	42	長崎 **Nagasaki**
11	埼玉 **Saitama**	27	大阪 **O-saka**	43	熊本 **Kumamoto**
12	千葉 **Chiba**	28	兵庫 **Hyo-go**	44	大分 **O-ita**
13	東京 **To-kyo-**	29	奈良 **Nara**	45	宮崎 **Miyazaki**
14	神奈川 **Kanagawa**	30	和歌山 **Wakayama**	46	鹿児島 **Kagoshima**
15	新潟 **Ni-gata**	31	鳥取 **Tottori**	47	沖縄 **Okinawa**

Colors

white しろ *shiro*	**light gray** ライトグレー *raito gure-*	**gray** グレー *gure-*
red あか *aka*	**pink** ピンク *pinku*	**vivid pink** ビビットピンク *bibitto pinku*
orange オレンジ *orenji*	**yellow** きいろ *ki-ro*	**lemon** レモンイエロー *remon iero-*
yellowish-green きみどり *kimidori*	**khaki** カーキ *ka-ki*	**green** みどり *midori*

light *akarui*   **dark** *kurai*

silver シルバー *shiruba-*	**gold** ゴールド *go-rudo*	**black** くろ *kuro*
dark red えんじ *enji*	**beige** ベージュ *be-ju*	**brown** ブラウン *buraun*
reddish-purple あかむらさき *aka murasaki*	**light purple** うすむらさき *usu murasaki*	**purple** むらさき *murasaki*
light blue みずいろ *mizuiro*	**blue** あお *ao*	**navy** こん *kon*

Greetings and Basic Words and Phrases

Good morning.
おはよう（おはようございます）
Ohayo- (Ohayo- gozaimasu)

Hello.
こんにちは
Konnichiwa

Good evening.
こんばんは
Konbanwa

Thank you.
ありがとう（ありがとうございます）
Arigato- (Arigato- gozaimasu)

Sorry.
ごめんなさい（申し訳ございません）
Gomen nasai (Mo-shiwake gozaimasen)

See you.
じゃあまた（失礼します）
Ja- mata (Shitsure- shimasu)

Yes. うん (はい)
Un (Hai)

No. ううん (いえ)
U-n (Ie)

When answering "yes", nod, and when answering "no", shake your head.

I understand.
わかりました
Wakarimashita

I don't understand.
わかりません
Wakarimasen

Making a circle with the thumb and forefinger means "okay", and tilting the head to the side is a gesture that means "Huh?"

Good night. おやすみなさい
Oyasumi nasai

The Japanese equivalent of "goodnight" is used, even when the listening is not about to go to sleep.

The following are phrases that are difficult to fully translate into English.

行ってきます
Itte kimasu

行ってらっしゃい
Itte rasshai

These are greetings used when people are leaving the house by the person leaving and the person still in the house.

ただいま
Tadaima

おかえりなさい
Okaeri nasai

These greetings are used when people come back home by the person returning and the person still in the house.

すみません
Sumimasen

This is a handy word that can be used to mean "excuse me", "sorry" and even "thank you."

いただきます
Itadakimasu

ごちそうさまです
Gochiso- samadesu

These are words that express gratitude used before and after eating. It is said while putting one's hands together in a prayer-like gesture. If the person who prepared the meal is present, it can be used to mean "Thank you for preparing this food." If they are not present, it can mean "Alright, let's eat."

Also, "Gochiso- samadesu" is can be said to restaurant employees when leaving after eating.

よろしく（よろしくお願いします）
Yoroshiku (Yoroshiku onegai shimasu)

This is a helpful expression that can be used in many different situations.

It can be used when asking for a favor, when introducing oneself and even as a closing line in an e-mail. When used with someone's name, like "[person's name] ni yoroshiku", it can mean "Please say hello to [person's name]."

Part 2

Survival

Learn about Japan by travelling in Japanese!

1 Shopping ①

008

1 I'd like to try this on.

2 How do you like it?

3 It's perfect.

4 It's a little small.

5 Do you have it in extra large?

6 I'd like to look around a bit more.

7 We would have to order the extra large size.

———Never mind, then.

Tips

If you would like to try something on, please notify
a store employee. They will remove the item from
its hanger and show you to the fitting room.
Most fitting rooms require that you remove your
shoes.

試着いいですか。
Shichaku i-desuka.

いかがでしたか。
Ikaga deshitaka.

ちょうどいいです。
Cho-do i-desu.

ちょっと小さいです。
Chotto chi-sai desu.

XLサイズありますか。
XLsaizu arimasuka.

ちょっと考えます。
Chotto kangaemasu.

XLサイズはおとりよせになります。
XLsaizuwa otoriyoseni narimasu.

——じゃあ、いいです。
ja-, i-desu.

009

Do you have a large one of this?

大きいのありますか。

O-ki-no arimasuka.

small
小さい
chi-sai

thick
厚い
atsui

shirt	**blouse**	**T-shirt**
シャツ	ブラウス	Tシャツ
shatsu	*burausu*	*T shatsu*

suit	**dress**	**a pair of hose**
スーツ	ワンピース	ストッキング
su-tsu	*wanpi-su*	*sutokkingu*

pants	**jeans**	**skirt**
ズボン	ジーンズ	スカート
zubon	*ji-nzu*	*suka-to*

shoes	**socks**	**belt**
くつ	くつした	ベルト
kutsu	*kutsushita*	*beruto*

long	short	cheap
長い	短い	安い
nagai	*mijikai*	*yasui*

thin
薄い
usui

It's a little expensive.
ちょっと高いです。
Chotto takaidesu

cardigan	jacket	coat
カーディガン	ジャケット	コート
ka-digan	*jaketto*	*ko-to*

tights	Kids'	Women's
タイツ	キッズ	レディース
taitsu	*kizzu*	*redi-su*

underwear
下着
shitagi

I'd like a men's sweater.
メンズのセーターがほしいです。
Menzu no se-ta- ga hoshi- desu.

bag
かばん
kaban

2 Shopping ②

🔊 010

1 How much is this?

2 Do you have any other colors?

3 I'd like this, please.

4 I'd like this, this, and this, please.

5 Is this for you (or someone else)?

——It's a gift.

6 Can I pay with a credit card?

7 Can I send it to America?

Tips

Most stores provide free gift wrapping,
so try asking the shop clerk.

これ、いくらですか。
Kore ikura desuka.

ほかの色はありますか。
Hoka no iro wa arimasuka.

これください。
Kore kudasai.

これと、これと、これください。
Kore to, kore to, kore kudasai.

ご自宅用ですか。
Gojitakuyo- desuka.

──プレゼントです。
Purezento desu.

クレジットカード使えますか。
Kurejittoka-do tsukaemasuka.

アメリカに配送できますか。
Amerika ni haiso- dekimasuka.

How much is this?

これいくらですか。

Kore ikura desuka.

rice cooker

炊飯器

suihanki

kettle

ケトル

ketoru

Please show me that.

それ見せてください。

Sore misete kudasai.

microwave oven

電子レンジ

denshirenji

speaker

スピーカー

supi-ka-

I'd like that.

あれください。

Are kudasai.

dryer

ドライヤー

doraiya-

wrist watch

腕時計

udedoke-

camera
カメラ
kamera

Can I try this?
これ、試せますか。
Kore, tamesemasuka.

computer
パソコン
pasokon

foundation
ファンデーション
fande-shon

mascara
マスカラ
masukara

T.V.
テレビ
terebi

eyebrow
アイブロウ
aiburou

eye liner
アイライナー
airaina-

air conditioner
エアコン
eakon

blush
チーク
chi-ku

lipstick
口紅
kuchibeni

vacuum cleaner
掃除機
so-jiki

lotion
化粧水
kesho-sui

milky lotion
乳液
nyu-eki

air purifier
空気清浄器
ku-kise-jo-ki

serum
美容液
biyo-eki

nail polish
マニキュア
manikyua

3 Convenience and Grocery Stores

🔊 012

1 Where is the gum?

2 Would you like me to microwave this?

——Yes, please.

3 Please wait one moment.

4 No bag, thank you.

5 I'd like a spoon, please.

6 Do you have a point card?

——No, I don't.

Tips

Convenience stores have a policy of putting hot and cold items in separate bags. They will also automatically provide things like chopsticks and spoons, so be sure to let them know if you don't need them.

ガムはどこですか。
Gamu wa doko desuka.

温めますか。
Atatamemasuka.

——お願いします。
Onegaishimasu.

少々お待ちください。
Sho-sho- omachi kudasai.

袋いりません。
Fukuro irimasen.

スプーンつけてください。
Supu-n tsukete kudasai.

ポイントカードお持ちですか。
Pointoka-do omochi desuka.

——ありません。
Arimasen.

Where is the milk.

牛乳どこにありますか。

Gyu-nyu- doko ni arimasuka.

water
お水
omizu

juice
ジュース
ju-su

chocolate	gum	mint
チョコレート	ガム	ミント
chokore-to	*gamu*	*minto*

sashimi (thinly-sliced raw fish)	natto (fermented soy beans)	umeboshi (dried salted plum)
刺身	納豆	梅ぼし
sashimi	*natto-*	*umeboshi*

tooth brush	dishwashing soap	laundry detergent
歯ブラシ	食器用洗剤	衣料用洗剤
haburashi	*shokkiyo-senzai*	*iryo-yo-senzai*

spoon	chopsticks	straw
スプーン	はし	ストロー
supu-n	*hashi*	*sutoro-*

tea
お茶
ocha

beer
ビール
bi-ru

whiskey
ウィスキー
wisuki-

Japanese sake
日本酒
nihonshu

shochu
焼酎
sho-chu-

wine
ワイン
wain

ham
ハム
hamu

bacon
ベーコン
be-kon

salad
サラダ
sarada

cheese
チーズ
chi-zu

bread
パン
pan

side dish
そうざい
so-zai

shampoo
シャンプー
shanpu-

conditioner
コンディショナー
kondishona-

soap
せっけん
sekken

hand towels
おてふき
otefuki

Please give me a fork.
フォークください。
Fo-ku kudasai.

 Cafés

🔊 014

① Do you have any menus in English?

② I'd like two medium hot coffees please.

③ To go, please. / For here, please.

④ Do you have anything without caffeine?

⑤ Non-smoking, please.

⑥ Would you like milk or sugar?

——Yes, please. / No, thank you.

——Just milk, please.

Tips

In Japan, decaffeinated products are called
"non kafein" or "kafeinresu".
But decaffeinated coffee is not yet caught on
in Japan.

英語のメニューありますか。
E-go no menyu- arimasuka.

Mサイズのホットコーヒー2つください。
M saizu no hottoko-hi- futatsu kudasai.

持ち帰りで。／こちらで。
Mochikaeri de. / Kochira de.

カフェインの入っていないものありますか。
Kafein no haitteinai mono arimasuka.

禁煙席でお願いします。
Kin'enseki de onegaishimasu.

》)⌒ お砂糖とミルクはいかがいたしますか。
Osato- to miruku wa ikagaitashimasuka.

――ください／大丈夫です。
Kudasai / Daijo-bu desu.

――ミルクだけください。
Miruku dake kudasai.

Two ice café lattes, please.

アイスカフェラテ2つください。

Aisukaferate futatsu kudasai.

hot
ホット
hotto

blend
ブレンド
burendo

milk
ミルク
miruku

sugar
さとう
sato-

lemon
レモン
remon

sandwich
サンドイッチ
sandoitchi

muffin
マフィン
mafin

croissant
クロワッサン
kurowassan

one (piece)
1つ
hitotsu

two (pieces)
2つ
futatsu

three (pieces)
3つ
mittsu

five (pieces)
5つ
itsutsu

six (pieces)
6つ
muttsu

seven (pieces)
7つ
nanatsu

ice アイス *aisu*	**coffee** コーヒー *ko-hi-*	**black tea** 紅茶 *ko-cha*
weak coffee アメリカン *amerikan*	**café latte** カフェラテ *kaferate*	**matcha latte** 抹茶ラテ *matcharate*
flan プリン *purin*	**donuts** ドーナツ *do-natsu*	**scone** スコーン *suko-n*
cheesecake チーズケーキ *chi-zuke-ki*	**chocolate cake** ガトーショコラ *gato-shokora*	**Mont Blanc** モンブラン *monburan*

four (pieces) 4つ *yottsu*	**counter** カウンター *kaunta-*	**table** テーブル *te-buru*
eight (pieces) 8つ *yattsu*	**Smoking, please.** 喫煙席で。 *Kitsuenseki de.*	

5 Restaurants

🔊 016

1 How many people are there in your party?

——Two people.

2 Is there any pork in this?

3 I can't eat meat.

4 I'm allergic to eggs.

5 Would you like your drinks after your meal?

——With the meal, please.

6 Check, please.

Tips

Labels mentioning the inclusion of shrimp, crab, wheat, buckwheat, eggs, milk and peanuts are now required on all food product packages. If you are not sure about something, try asking.

何名様ですか。
Nanme-sama desuka.

──2人です。
Futari desu.

これ、豚肉は入ってますか。
Kore, butaniku wa haittemasuka.

肉が食べられません。
Niku ga taberaremasen.

卵アレルギーです。
Tamago arerugi- desu.

お飲み物はお食事の後でよろしいでしょうか。
Onomimono wa oshokuji no ato de yoroshi-desho-ka.

──いっしょにください。
Issho ni kudasai.

お会計お願いします。
Okaike- onegaishimasu.

017

I'm allergic to shrimp.

えびアレルギーです。

Ebi arerugi- desu.

egg
卵
tamago

milk
乳（牛乳）
nyu- (gyu-nyu-)

pork
豚肉
butaniku

beef
牛肉
gyu-niku

chicken
鶏肉
toriniku

cashew nut
カシューナッツ
kashu-nattsu

walnut
くるみ
kurumi

soy bean
大豆
daizu

Seven people.

7人です。

Nananin desu.

one person
1人
hitori

three people
3人
san'nin

flour
小麦
komugi

sesami seed
ごま
goma

crab
かに
kani

salmon
さけ
sake

mackerel
さば
saba

salmon roe
いくら
ikura

meat
肉類
nikurui

raw fish
生魚
namazakana

gelatin
ゼラチン
zerachin

fruit
果物
kudamono

I can't eat peanut.

落花生が食べられません。
rakkase- ga taberaremasen.

two people
2人
futari

four people
4人
yonin

five people
5人
gonin

six people
6人
rokunin

6 Clinics

018

1 I feel nauseous.

2 My head hurts.

3 I feel sick.

4 My appetite is gone.

5 I have a fever.

6 I'm itchy.

7 Since when (have you had these symptoms)?

——Since yesterday.

Tips

In Japan, after receiving medical examinations
and prescriptions from hospitals,
you are free to choose your own pharmacy.

吐き気がします。
Hakike ga shimasu.

頭が痛いです。
Atama ga itai desu.

気分が悪いです。
Kibun ga warui desu.

食欲がありません。
Shokuyoku ga arimasen.

熱があります。
Netsu ga arimasu.

かゆいです。
Kayui desu.

いつからですか。
Itsu kara desuka.

──昨日からです。
Kino- kara desu.

019

Are there any people who can speak English?
英語の話せる方いますか。
E-go no hanaseru kata imasuka.

doctor
先生
sense-

nurse
看護士さん
kangoshisan

nausea
はきけ
hakike

dizziness
めまい
memai

palpitations
どうき
do-ki

I'm shivering.
寒気がします。
Samuke ga shimasu.

ringing in the ears
耳なり
miminari

dentistry
歯科
shika

ophthalmology
眼科
ganka

internal medicine
内科
naika

reception
受付
uketsuke

pharmacy
薬局
yakkyoku

cosmetic surgery
整形外科
se-ke-geka

high blood pressure
高血圧
ko-ketsuatsu

I'm pregnant.
妊娠中です。
Ninshinchu- desu.

low blood pressure
低血圧
te-ketsuatsu

receiving treatment
治療中
chiryo-chu-

having one's period
生理中
se-richu-

mucus, snot
はな
hana

I'm sweating.
汗が出ます。
Ase ga demasu.

sneeze
くしゃみ
kushami

cough
せき
seki

phlegm
たん
tan

dermatology
皮膚科
hifuka

Where is the surgery department?
外科はどこですか
Geka wa doko desuka.

urology
泌尿器科
hinyo-kika

pediatrics
小児科
sho-nika

obstetrics and gynecology
産婦人科
sanfujinka

 Pharmacies

🔊 020

1. **Do you have your prescription?**

2. **I'd like some headache medicine.**

3. **I'd like the generic version, please.**

4. **Will this make me drowsy?**

5. **Take this three times a day after every meal.**

6. **Take it within 30 minutes of eating.**

7. **Take two pills each time.**

8. **Please take care.**

Tips

Generic drugs are licensed drugs that are more affordable versions of newer drugs that have the same active ingredients and effects. If no special requests are made, the newer version of drugs will be prescribed.

処方箋お持ちですか。
Shoho-sen omochi desuka.

頭痛薬が欲しいんですが。
Zutsu-yaku ga hoshi-ndesuga.

ジェネリックでお願いします。
Jenerikku de onegaishimasu.

これ、飲むと眠くなりますか。
Kore, nomu to nemuku narimasuka.

1日3回、毎食後に飲んでください。
Ichinichi san kai, maishokugo ni nonde kudasai.

食後30分以内に飲んでください。
Shokugo sanjuppun inai ni nonde kuasai.

1回2錠飲んでください。
Ikkai nijo- nonde kudasai.

おだいじに。
Odaijini.

I'd like some cold medicine.

風邪の薬ください。

Kaze no kusuri kudasai.

headache
頭痛
zutsu-

heartburn
胸焼け
muneyake

motion sickness
乗り物酔い
norimonoyoi

injury, wound
傷
kizu

burn
やけど
yakedo

cough lozenge
トローチ
toro-chi

cough drop
のどあめ
nodoame

eye medicine
目薬
megusuri

gauze
ガーゼ
ga-ze

adhesive bandage
ばんそうこう
banso-ko-

compress
しっぷ
shippu

antiseptic
消毒液
sho-dokueki

mask
マスク
masuku

thermometer
体温計
taionke-

stomachache 腹痛 *fukutsu-*	**menstrual pain** 生理痛 *se-ritsu-*	**cold** 風邪 *kaze*
hangover 二日酔い *futsukayoi*	**diarrhea** 下痢 *geri*	**constipation** 便秘 *benpi*
gastroenteritis 胃腸炎 *icho-en*	**anemia** 貧血 *hinketsu*	**dry skin** 肌荒れ *hada are*

powder medicine 粉薬 *konagusuri*	**pill** 錠剤 *jo-zai*	**capsule** カプセル *kapuseru*
every meal 毎食 *maishoku*	**before retiring** 就寝前 *shu-shinmae*	**every three hours** 3時間毎 *sanjikan goto*
before a meal 食前 *shokuzen*	**between meals** 食間 *shokkan*	**after a meal** 食後 *shokugo*

8 The Post Office and The Bank

🔊 022

1 Please take a numbered ticket.

2 I'd like five postcards, please.

3 Three 82-yen stamps, please.

4 I'd like this sent by ordinary mail, please.

5 Please have this delivered in the quickest method possible.

6 About when will it arrive?

7 I'd like to exchange some money.

8 I'd like to open an account.

Tips

Addresses on packages being sent to places
in Japan can be written in Roman characters
and they will still arrive. Domestic delivery
postcards cost 52 yen, while envelopes can
be sent for 82 yen or more.

整理券をお取りください。
Se-riken o otorikudasai.

ハガキ5枚お願いします。
Hagaki gomai onegaishimasu.

82円切手3枚ください。
Hachiju-nien kitte sanmai kudasai.

普通郵便でお願いします。
Futsu- yu-bin de onegaishimasu.

一番早いのにしてください。
Ichiban hayaino ni shitekudasai.

いつごろ着きますか。
Itsugoro tsukimasuka.

両替したいのですが。
Ryo-gae shitai no desuga.

口座を開きたいのですが。
Ko-za o hirakitai no desuga.

Express mail, please.
速達で。
Sokutatsu de.

regular mail
普通郵便
Futsu-yu-bin

air mail
航空便
ko-ku-bin

deposit 入金 *nyu-kin*	remittance, sending money 送金 *so-kin*	withdrawal 引き出し *hikidashi*
savings 預金 *yokin*	balance inquiry 残高照会 *zandakasho-kai*	payment 支払い *shiharai*

foreign currency 外貨 *gaika*	yen 円 *en*	dollar ドル *doru*
won ウォン *won*	yuan 元 *gen*	baht バーツ *ba-tsu*

insured
保険付
hokentsuki

economy service (Surface Air Lifted)
SAL便
saru bin

express mail service
EMS
i- emu esu

sea mail
船便
funabin

registered mail
書留
kakitome

international parcel post
国際小包
kokusaikozutumi

opening an account
口座開設
ko-zakaisetsu

I want to exchange this for Japanese yen.
円に両替したいです。
En ni ryo-gae shitaidesu.

registry, entry
記帳
kicho-

euro
ユーロ
yu-ro

dong
ドン
don

rouble
ルーブル
ru-buru

peso
ペソ
peso

real
レアル
rearu

rupiah
ルピア
rupia

 Trains

🔊 024

1 I'm trying to get to Asakusa.

2 Please take the Ginza Line headed to Asakusa.

3 It's platform number 2.

4 It's station G 09.

5 What color is the line?

——It's the orange line.

6 Do I have to make any transfers?

——You need to transfer at Ueno Station.

Tips

Train lines in Tokyo are designated by color,
for example, the Ginza Line is orange and the
Tozai Line is blue.

浅草に行きたいんですが。
Asakusa ni ikitaindesuga.

銀座線の浅草行きに乗ってください。
Ginzasen no Asakusa iki ni nottekudasai.

２番ホームです。
Niban ho-mu desu.

Ｇ09の駅ですよ。
G kyu- no eki desuyo.

何色のラインですか?
Nani iro no rain desuka.

――オレンジのラインです。
Orenji no rain desu.

乗り換えはありますか。
Norikae wa arimasuka.

――上野駅で乗り換えです。
Uenoeki de norikae desu.

One limited express ticket, please.

特急券ください。

Tokkyu-ken kudasai.

reserved seat ticket
指定席券
Shite-sekiken

IC card
ICカード
ai shi- ka-do

accident 事故 *jiko*	malfunction, breakdown, failure 故障 *kosho-*	delay 遅延 *chien*
inbound 上り *nobori*	outbound 下り *kudari*	last train/bus 最終 *saishu-*
bound for ~ ~行き *iki*	stopping at ~ ~方面 *ho-men*	departing from ~ ~発 *hatsu*
local train 各駅停車 *kakuekite-sha*	regular train 普通 *futsu-*	rapid train 快速 *kaisoku*

first-class ticket グリーン券 *guri-nsha*	**coupon ticket** 回数券 *kaisu-ken*	**tour ticket** 周遊券 *shu-yu-ken*

commuter pass
定期券
te-kiken

"operation cancellation"
「運転見合わせ」
untenmiawase

out of service
回送
kaiso-

first train/bus 始発 *shihatsu*	**operation suspended** 運転中止 *untenchu-shi*	**resuming operation** 運転再開 *untensaikai*
arriving at ~ ~着 *chaku*	**car number ~** ~号車 *go-sha*	**vehicle number** ~両目 *ryo-me*
local express train 準急 *junkyu-*	**express train** 急行 *kyu-ko-*	**limited express train** 特急 *tokkyu-*

Topic

10 The Shinkansen

◀ 026

1. Two adult tickets to Shin-Osaka, please.

2. There is unreserved and reserved seating.

——Reserved seating, please.

3. What kind of seats would you like?

——A window seat, please.

——A seat where I can see Mt. Fuji.

4. May I see your tickets?

5. May I put my seat back?

Tips

When travelling on the Shinkansen from
Tokyo to Nagoya, Kyoto or Osaka, if you
are seated on the right-hand side, you can
see Mt. Fuji.

大人二人、新大阪までお願いします。
Otona futari, Shin'o-saka made onegaishimasu.

自由席と指定席がございます。
Jiyu-seki to shite-seki gozaimasu.

――指定席にしてください。
Shite-seki ni shitekudasai.

座席の希望ございますか。
Zaseki no kibo- gozaimasuka.

――窓側で。
Madogawa de.

――富士山の見える方で。
Fujisan no mieru ho- de.

切符を拝見します。
Kippu o haiken shimasu.

（背もたれを）倒してもいいですか？
(Semotare o) taoshitemo iidesuka.

front 一番前の *ichiban mae no*	**rear** 一番後ろの *ichiban ushiro no*	**near the bathroom** トイレ付近の *toire fukin no*
widow-side 窓側の *madogawa no*	**aisle-side** 通路側の *tsu-rogawa no*	**chargeable** 充電のできる *ju-den no dekiru*

Where is the ticket gate?

改札はどこですか。

Kaisatsu wa doko desuka.

north entrance 北口 *kitaguchi*	
entrance 入口 *iriguchi*	

station office 駅事務室 *eki jimushitsu*	**locker** ロッカー *rokka-*	**kiosk** キオスク *kiosuku*
stairs 階段 *kaidan*	**elevator** エレベーター *erebe-ta-*	**escalator** エスカレーター *esukare-ta-*

two-seater
2人掛けの
futarigake no

mountain-viewing side
山側の
yamagawa no

I'd like a seat facing the ocean.

海側の席にしてください。

Umigawa no seki ni shite kudasai.

west entrance
西口
nishiguchi

south entrance
南口
minamiguchi

east entrance
東口
higashiguchi

exit
出口
deguchi

connecting terminal
連絡口
renrakuguchi

central entrance
中央口
chu-o-guchi

ticket counter
きっぷ売り場
kippuuriba

fare adjustment machine

「精算機」

se-sanki

ticket machine
券売機
kenbaiki

Taxis and Buses

🔊 028

1 How much to get to Tokyo Station?

2 Does this bus go to Asakusa Station?

3 To Hotel ABC, please.

4 Can you put my luggage in the trunk, please?

5 How long will it take?

6 Take a right at the next light.

7 Take a left at the next intersection.

8 Please stop there.

Tips

Most buses that run in cities like Tokyo and Kyoto have a set fair. All-day passes are available for sightseeing, so ask the information desk or the driver about them.

東京駅まで、いくらかかりますか。
To-kyo- made, ikura kakarimasuka.

このバスは浅草駅に行きますか。
Kono basu wa asakusaeki ni ikimasuka.

ABCホテルまでお願いします。
ABC hoteru made onegaishimasu.

荷物をトランクに積んでもらえますか。
Nimotsu o toranku ni tsunde moraemasuka.

何分くらいかかりますか。
Nanpun kurai kakarimasuka.

次の信号を右です。
Tsugi no shingo- o migi desu.

次の交差点を左です。
Tsugi no ko-saten o hidari desu.

あそこで停めてください。
Asoko de tometekudasai.

To this address, please.

この住所までお願いします。

Kono ju-sho made onegaishimasu.

JR station
JRの駅
JR no eki

Metro station
地下鉄の駅
chikatetsu no eki

traffic light
信号
shingo-

corner
角
kado

pedestrian crossing
横断歩道
o-danhodo-

intersection
交差点
ko-saten

pedestrian bridge
歩道橋
hodo-kyo-

ahead
先
saki

Please stop in front of the building.

建物の前に停めてください。

Tatemono no mae ni tomete kudasai.

left-hand side
左手
hidarite

center
中
naka

closest bus station 最寄のバス停 *moyori no basute-*	# One taxi, please. タクシー1台お願いします。 *Takushi- ichidai onegaishimasu.*
airport 空港 *ku-ko-*	# One taxi for tomorrow morning at 7:00, please. 明日の朝7時に1台お願いします。 *Ashita no asa shichiji ni ichidai onegaishimasu.*
sign 看板 *kanban*	# The address is... 住所は・・・です。 *Ju-sho wa ... desu.*
next to となり *tonari*	# My destination is... 行先は・・・です。 *Ikisaki wa ... desu.*
right-hand side 右手 *migite*	# Thank you. (lit. I am asking kindly for your help.) よろしくお願いします。 *Yoroshiku onegaishimasu.*
below 下 *shita*	

73

 Hotels

🔊 030

1 I'd like to check in.

2 Is there Internet access available?

3 Can I leave my luggage here?

4 What time is breakfast?

5 Could you call me a taxi at 8:00?

6 I'd like a wake-up call at 7:00.

7 My room is cold.

8 The bathroom robe is too small.

Tips

Recently, many business hotels offer a
choice of pillows and cell phone chargers
or humidifiers for rent. It might be fun to
stay at a business hotel some time.

チェックインお願いします。
Chekkuin onegaishimasu.

ネットは使えますか。
Netto wa tsukaemasuka.

荷物預けられますか。
Nimotsu azukeraremasuka.

朝食は何時からですか。
Cho-shoku wa nanji kara desuka.

8時にタクシーを呼んでもらえますか。
Hachiji ni takushi- o yonde moraemasuka.

7時にモーニングコールをお願いします。
Shichiji ni mo-ninguko-ru o onegaishimasu.

部屋が寒いんですが。
Heya ga samuindesuga.

部屋着が小さいんですが。
Heyagi ga chiisaindesuga.

I'd like to reserve a room.
部屋の予約お願いします。
Heya no yoyaku onegaishimasu.

check-in
チェックイン
chekkuin

room service
ルームサービス
ru-musa-bisu

room with a single bed
シングル
shinguru

room for two people
ダブル
daburu

room with twin beds
ツイン
tsuin

front desk
フロント
furonto

elevator
エレベーター
erebe-ta-

bar
バー
ba-

restaurant
レストラン
resutoran

cafeteria
食堂
shokudo-

bath
お風呂
ofuro

Where is the vending machine?
自販機はどこですか。
Jihanki wa doko desuka.

restroom, toilet
トイレ
toire

check-out
チェックアウト
chekkuauto

change the reservation time
予約時間の変更
yoyaku jikan no henko-

reservation cancellation
予約のキャンセル
yoyaku no kyanseru

wake-up call
モーニングコール
mo-ninguko-ru

Western-style room
洋室
yo-shitsu

Japanese-style room
和室
washitsu

one night
1泊
ippaku

two nights
2泊
nihaku

three nights
3泊
sanpaku

four nights
4泊
yonhaku

five nights
5泊
gohaku

six nights
6泊
roppaku

slippers
スリッパ
surippa

I'd like a new set of sheets, please.
シーツの交換お願いします。
Shi-tsu no ko-kan onegaishimasu.

bath towel
バスタオル
basutaoru

pillow
まくら
makura

bath robe
部屋着
heyagi

13 Room Renting and Homestays

1 Thank you for letting me stay here.

2 Where can I smoke?

3 Where can I throw this away?

4 I'd like to borrow a refrigerator.

5 Could you tell me the Wi-Fi password?

6 Where should I return the key?

7 I'd like to extend my visit.

8 Thank you for your hospitality.

Tips

When going out in Japan, it is customary to carry any trash with you home and throw it away there, so there are no trashcans on the street. Methods of trash disposal vary from city to city.

お世話になります。
Osewani narimasu.

どこで煙草が吸えますか。
Doko de tabako ga suemasuka.

これはどこに捨てますか。
Kore wa doko ni sutemasuka.

冷蔵庫を借りたいです。
Re-zo-ko o karitaidesu.

Wi-Fiのパスワードを教えてください。
Waifai no pasuwa-do o oshiete kudasai.

鍵はどこに返せばいいですか。
Kagi wa doko ni kaeseba iidesuka.

延泊したいのですが。
Enpaku shitaino desuga.

お世話になりました。
Osewani narimashita.

I'd like to borrow a refrigerator.

冷蔵庫貸してください。
Re-zo-ko kashite kudasai.

microwave
電子レンジ
denshirenji

washing machine
洗濯機
sentakuki

pen
ペン
pen

towel
タオル
taoru

Japanese quilted mattress
布団
futon

combustible waste
もえるごみ
moeru gomi

non-combustible waste
もえないごみ
moenai gomi

can
かん
kan

oversized garbage
粗大ごみ
sodaigomi

plastic
プラ
pura

bottle
びん
bin

Is this recyclable waste?

これは資源ごみですか。
Kore wa shigengomi desuka.

PET bottle
ペットボトル
pettobotoru

umbrella	shower	phone
かさ	シャワー	電話
kasa	*shawa-*	*denwa*

cup/glass	tableware	kitchen
コップ／グラス	食器	キッチン
koppu / gurasu	*shokki*	*kitchin*

blanket	heater	(electric) fan
毛布	ストーブ	扇風機
mo-fu	*suto-bu*	*senpu-ki*

the sheets are dirty	There's no hot water.
シーツが汚い	お湯が出ないんですが。
shi-tsu ga kitanai	*Oyu ga denaindesuga.*

the Internet isn't working	the room next door is too loud
ネットがつながらない	となりの部屋がうるさい
netto ga tsunagaranai	*tonari no heya ga urusai*

the air condition is broken	the door won't lock
エアコンがきかない	鍵が閉まらない
eakon ga kikanai	*kagi ga shimaranai*

Me and My Family

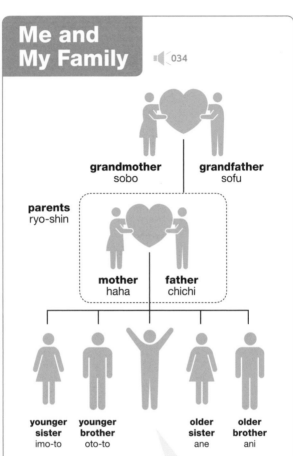

🔊 034

grandmother
sobo

grandfather
sofu

parents
ryo-shin

mother
haha

father
chichi

younger sister
imo-to

younger brother
oto-to

older sister
ane

older brother
ani

Ways of saying "I"

Everyone from small children to elderly men used the term "watashi." It can also be used in formal settings. In business or polite speaking situations, "watakushi" can also be used. The term "boku" is used mostly be men.It is somewhat casual. "Ore" is used primarily by young men and is very casual.

Part 3

Communication

May your best souvenirs from Japan be the memories you make with Japanese friends

1 Sightseeing

🔊 035

1 Could you take my picture?

2 Please get the building in the picture, too.

3 Okay, cheese!

4 Are there any ATMs nearby?

5 May I use your bathroom?

6 Is Kiyomizu-dera within walking distance?

7 Which way is the station?

8 Please take off your shoes.

Tips

When taking pictures in Japan, the majority
of people take them on the last sound of
the phrase "Hai, chiizu!" (Cheese!). Others
countdown "San, ni, ichi! (Three, two, one!)."

写真お願いできますか。
Shashin onegai dekimasuka.

建物を入れてください。
Tatemono o irete kudasai.

はい、チーズ!
Hai, chi-zu!

この近くにATMありますか。
Kono chikaku ni ATM arimasuka.

トイレ貸してください。
Toire kashite kudasai.

清水寺には歩いて行けますか。
Kiyomizudera niwa aruite ikemasuka.

駅はどっちですか。
Eki wa dotchi desuka.

))) 靴を脱いでください。
Kutsu o nuide kudasai.

036

Are there any convenience stores nearby?

近くにコンビニありますか。

Chikaku ni konbini arimasuka.

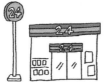

supermarket
スーパー
su-pa-

hospital
病院
byo-in

---

eat here
ここで食べて
koko de tabete

drink here
ここで飲んで
koko de nonde

take a break
休んで
yasunde

take pictures
写真を撮って
shashin o totte

touch
さわって
sawatte

borrow a chair
いすを借りて
isu o karite

Could you take one more, please?

もう一枚とってもらえませんか。

Mo- ichimai totte moraemasenka.

take it horizontally
横でとって
yoko de totte

call a taxi
タクシーを呼んで
takushi- o yonde

police box 交番 *ko-ban*	**sightseeing information desk** 観光案内所 *kanko-an'naijo*	**restroom, toilet** トイレ *toire*
pharmacy 薬局 *yakkyoku*	**station** 駅 *eki*	**bus stop** バス停 *basute-*

make a call
電話して
denwashite

use a power outlet
コンセント使って
konsento tsukatte

Can I enter with my shoes on.

このまま入っていいですか。

Konomama haitte i-desuka.

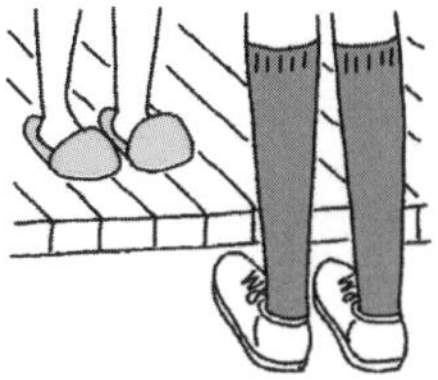

take it vertically 縦でとって *tate de totte*	**include the background** 背景をいれて *haike- o irete*	**take it up close** 近くでとって *chikaku de totte*
interpret 通訳して *tsu-yakushite*	**draw a map** 地図を書いて *chizu o kaite*	**show me the way** 案内して *an'naishite*

2 Formal Introductions

 037

1 Nice to meet you.

2 My name is Dianna.

3 Please call me D.

4 I came from America.

5 What do you do for a living?

　　——I work at a company.

6 Nice to meet you.

7 Thank you very much.
　　* When you receive one's card.

Tips

When adults greet one another, business cards
are often presented. When introducing yourself,
hand the other person your business card using
two hands.

はじめまして。
Hajimemashite.

Diannaと申します。
Dianna to mo-shimasu.

Dと呼んでください。
D to yonde kudasai.

アメリカから参りました。
Amerika kara mairimashita.

ご職業は。
Goshokugyo- wa.

——会社員です。
Kaishain desu.

よろしくお願いします。
Yoroshiku onegaisimasu.

頂戴いたします。
Cho-dai itashimasu.

I'm a teacher.

教師です。

Kyo-shi desu.

elementary school student
小学生
sho-gakuse-

company worker
会社員
kaishain

programmer
プログラマー
purogurama-

engineer
エンジニア
enjinia

police officer
警察官
ke-satsukan

driver
運転手
untenshu

artisan
職人
shokunin

chef
料理人
ryo-rinin

camera person
カメラマン
kameraman

consultant
コンサルタント
konsarutanto

performer
パフォーマー
pafo-ma-

self-employed person
自営業
jie-gyo-

freelance worker
フリーランス
furi-ransu

part-time worker
アルバイト
arubaito

junior high school school student	high school stident	university student
中学生	高校生	大学生
chu-gakuse-	*ko-ko-se-*	*daigakuse-*

temporary employee	public servant	graduate school student
派遣	公務員	大学院生
haken	*ko-muin*	*daigakuinse-*

architect	beautician	researcher
設計士	美容師	研究者
sekke-shi	*biyo-shi*	*kenkyu-sha*

fire fighter	doctor	nurse
消防士	医者	看護士
sho-bo-shi	*isha*	*kangoshi*

reporter	care worker	childcare giver
記者	介護士	保育士
kisha	*kaigoshi*	*hoikushi*

housewife	looking for a job	backpacker
主婦	求職中	バックパッカー
shufu	*kyu-shokuchu-*	*bakkupakka-*

91

3 Casual Introductions

🔊 039

1 I'm Diana.

2 What should I call you?

——Call me D.

3 Where're you from?

——I'm from Chicago in America.

4 How old are you?

——Twenty six this year.

5 Nice to meet you.

Tips

Titles in Japan can be complicated, but in general, remember that boys are referred to as "-kun", girls are referred to as "-chan", and everyone else can be called "-san."

Diannaです。
Dianna desu.

何て呼んだらいい？
Nante yondara i-?

──D って呼んで。
Dtte yonde.

出身は？
Shusshin wa?

──アメリカの、シカゴ出身。
Amerika no, Shikago shusshin.

歳は？
Toshi wa?

──今年26歳。
Kotoshi niju-roku sai.

よろしくね。
Yoroshikune.

I like basketball!

バスケが好き!

Basuke ga suki!

jogging
ジョギング
Jogingu

baseball
野球
yakyu-

rock
ロック
rokku

classical
クラシック
kurashikku

jazz
ジャズ
jazu

folk
フォーク
fo-ku

rap
ラップ
rappu

guitar
ギター
gita-

movie
映画
e-ga

cooking
料理
ryo-ri

travel
旅行
ryoko-

job, work
仕事
shigoto

reading
読書
dokusho

eating tour
食べ歩き
tabearuki

soccer サッカー *sakka-*	**hockey** ホッケー *hokke-*	**sports** スポーツ *supo-tsu*
swimming 水泳 *suie-*	**tennis** テニス *tenisu*	**mountain hiking** 登山 *tozan*

pop
ポップ
poppu

Do you like Japanese music?
日本の音楽は好き?
Nihon no ongaku wa suki?

piano
ピアノ
piano

walking 散歩 *sanpo*	**car** 車 *kuruma*	**computer** パソコン *pasokon*
yoga ヨガ *yoga*	**picture** 写真 *shashin*	**game** ゲーム *ge-mu*

Topic

4 Social Media

🔊 041

1 Do you have LINE?

—Yes, I do.
/ No, I don't.

2 Can I friend you?

3 Can you enter your info?

4 Can you read QR codes?

5 How do you spell that?

6 How do you write "Sayuri?"

7 I just sent it.

Tips

LINE is a social networking service that was created in Japan. You can use it to make calls and send messages.

LINEやってる?
LINE yatteru?

——やってる。／やってない。
Yatteru./Yattenai.

ともだちになっていい?
Tomodachini natte i-?

入力してもらっていい?
Nyu-ryoku shitemoratte -?

QRコード読める?
QR ko-do yomeru?

スペルおしえて。
Superu oshiete.

「さゆり」ってどう書くの?
Sayuritte do-kakuno?

いま送ったよ。
Ima okuttayo.

042

This picture is so cute!
写真かわいいね!
Shashin kawai-ne!

beautiful
きれい
kire-

awesome/ lovely
素敵
suteki

What is your partner like?
パートナーどんな人?
pa-tona- donna hito?

wife
奥さん
okusan

sympathetic やさしい *yasashi-*	**serious** まじめ *majime*	**smart** 頭いい *atamai-*
laidback おっとり *ottori*	**impatient** せっかち *sekkachi*	**rich** お金持ち *okanemochi*
a hard worker 仕事熱心 *shigoto nesshin*	**moody** 気分屋 *kibun ya*	**selfish** わがまま *wagamama*

cool かっこいい *kakkoi-*	**funny/ interesting** おもしろい *omoshiroi*	**wonderful/ amazing** すごい *sugoi*
stylish/ fashionable おしゃれ *oshare*	**Who is this person?** この人だれ? *konohito dare?*	
husband 旦那さん *dannasan*	**girlfriend** 彼女 *kanojo*	**boyfriend** 彼氏 *kareshi*
stupid ばか *baka*	**generous** 気前がいい *kimaegai-*	**stingy** けち *kechi*
poor 貧乏 *binbo-*	**talkative** おしゃべり *oshaberi*	**quiet** しずか *shizuka*
(physically) strong 力持ち *chikaramochi*	**I'm good at cooking.** 料理上手だよ。 *Ryo-rijo-zu dayo.*	

5 Medical Condition

043

1 How are you?

——I'm good.

2 I think I have a cold.

3 You don't look so good.

4 You okay?

——I've been pretty busy lately.

——I didn't get much sleep.

5 Take care of yourself.

Tips

Standard Western greetings like this are not
commonly used in Japan. When talking to
someone they see daily, most people
instead talk about the weather.

元気?
Genki?

——うん、元気。
Un, genki.

風邪気味。
Kazegimi.

顔色よくないね。
Kaoiro yokunaine.

大丈夫?
Daijo-bu?

——最近いそがしい。
Saikin isogashi-.

——寝不足で。
Nebusoku de.

おだいじにね。
Odaijinine.

044

How are you doing?
調子どう?
Cho-shi do-?

in good spirits, healthy
元気
genki

eating
食べてる
tabeteru

Same as always.
いつも通りだよ。
Itsumodo-ri dayo.

exercising
運動してる
undo- shiteru

found a boyfriend/ girlfriend
恋人できた
koibito dekita

making the most of
充実してる
ju-jitsu shiteru

caught a cold
風邪ひいた
kaze hi-ta

running out of money
金欠
kinketsu

favorable, going all right
順調
juncho-

taking a break, taking time off
休んでる
yasunderu

lost weight, got thin
やせた
yaseta

sleeping 寝てる *neteru*	**Great!** よかったね! *Yokatta ne!*
studying 勉強してる *benkyo- shiteru*	**Really?** ほんとに? *Honto ni?*
busy 忙しい *isogashi-*	**Why?** なんで? *Nande?*
free, not busy ひま *hima*	**Me, too.** わたしも。 *Watashi mo.*
travelling 旅行してる *ryoko- shiteru*	**That's true.** だよね。 *Dayone.*
gained weight, got fat 太った *futotta*	**Are you okay?** 大丈夫? *Daijo-bu?*

The Weather

🔊 045

1 It's warm out today.

2 The weather is clear for the first time in a while.

3 Is it raining/snowing now?

4 There's been nothing but rain lately.

5 It's gotten pretty cool.

6 It's fall through and through.

7 It's hot and humid.

8 I can't stop sweating.

Tips

Japanese are particularly sensitive to the changing of the seasons, and talking about the weather is used in place of greetings.

今日は暖かいですね。
Kyo- wa atatakai desune.

久しぶりに晴れましたね。
Hisashiburi ni haremashitane.

今降ってますか。
Ima futtemasuka.

最近雨ばっかりですね。
Saikin ame bakkari desune.

涼しくなりましたね。
Suzushiku narimashitane.

すっかり秋ですね。
Sukkari akidesune.

蒸し暑いですね。
Mushiatsui desune.

汗が止まりません。
Ase ga tomarimasen.

Is it hot today?

今日は暑いですか。

Kyo- wa atsui desuka.

hot and humid

蒸し暑い

mushi atsui

high humidity

湿度が高い

shitsudo ga takai

UV rays are strong

紫外線が強い

shigaisen ga tsuyoi

a lot of pollen

花粉が多い

kafun ga o-i

clear weather

晴れ

hare

Do I need a coat today?

今日コートいりますか。

kyo- ko-to irimasuka.

raincoat

レインコート

reinko-to

sunblock, sunscreen

日焼けどめ

hiyakedome

parasol

日傘

higasa

umbrella

傘

kasa

cardigan

カーディガン

ka-digan

gloves

手袋

tebukuro

scarf, muffler

マフラー

mafura-

warm 暖かい *atatakai*	**cool** 涼しい *suzushi-*	**cold** 寒い *samui*
just right ちょうどいい *cho-do i-*	**feeling good, feeling pleasant** 気持ちいい *kimochi i-*	**the wind is strong** 風が強い *kaze ga tsuyoi*
rain 雨 *ame*	**cloudy, cloudiness** くもり *kumori*	**thunder, lightning** 雷 *kaminari*

spring 春 *haru*	**This weather feels like it's the rainy season.** 梅雨らしい天気ですね。 *Tsuyu rashi- tenki desune.*	
summer 夏 *natsu*	**fall, autumn** 秋 *aki*	**winter** 冬 *fuyu*
Okinawa 沖縄 *Okinawa*	**October** 10月 *ju-gatsu*	**New Year's Day** 正月 *sho-gatsu*

7 Making Calls

🔊 047

1. **Hello. This is Dianna.**

2. **I can't hear you so well.**

3. **Can you repeat that?**

4. **Please speak slowly.**

5. **May I ask who's speaking?**

6. **This is Smith. You called earlier.**

7. **Thank you for your continued support.**

8. **I'm sorry, I made a mistake.**

Tips

Japanese frequently bow when saying things like "arigato (thank you)" and "sumimasen (excuse me)." Often times, many people even bow when talking on the phone, even though the other person can't see them.

もしもし、Diannaです。
Moshimoshi, Dianna desu.

よく聞こえません。
Yoku kikoemasen.

もう一度お願いします。
Mouichido onegaishimasu.

ゆっくりお願いします。
Yukkuri onegaishimasu.

どなたでしょうか。
Donata desho-ka.

お電話いただいたSmithです。
Odenwa itadaita Smith desu.

お世話になっております。
Osewani natteorimasu.

すみません、間違えました。
Sumimasen, machigaemashita.

⑧ Making Reservations

🔊 048

① I'd like to make a reservation.

② Do you have any openings tomorrow afternoon.

——We're full in the afternoon.

③ We're booked solid.

④ How about in the morning?

⑤ Then, 10:00, please.

——Yes, sir/ma'am.

⑥ We will see you then.

Tips

More and more stores like restaurants and hair salons are offering online reservations. It might be worth checking out if a phone isn't readily available.

予約をしたいんですが。
Yoyaku o shitaindesuga.

明日の午後は空いていますか？
Ashita no gogo wa aiteimasuka?

))⌒ ——午後はいっぱいです。
Gogo wa ippai desu.

))⌒ 予約で埋まっています。
Yoyaku de umatteimasu.

))⌒ 午前中はいかがでしょうか。
Gozenchu- wa ikaga desho-ka.

じゃあ10時でお願いします。
Ja- ju-ji de onegaishimasu.

))⌒ ——かしこまりました。
Kashikomarimashita.

))⌒ お待ちしております。
Omachishite orimasu.

Beauty Salons

049

1 Hello. I have a reservation under the name Smith.

2 Please have a seat here.

3 How much would you like to have cut?

——Five centimeters, please.

4 About this much?

5 It's a little too long.

6 What would you like to do with your bangs?

——There okay as they are.

Tips

If you can't communicate in Japanese, try showing them a picture on your smart phone.

こんにちは、予約したSmithです。
Kon'nichiwa, yoyaku shita Smith desu.

))) こちらでかけてお待ちください。
Kochira de kakete omachikudasai.

))) どれくらい切りますか。
Dore kurai kirimasuka.

——5センチくらい切ってください。
Gosenchi kurai kitte kudasai.

))) これくらいでしょうか。
Kore kurai desho-ka.

——少し長すぎます。
Sukoshi nagasugimasu.

))) 前髪はどうしますか。
Maegami wa do-shimasuka.

——そのままで。
Sonomama de.

050

I'd like a cut and shampoo, please.
カットとシャンプーお願いします。
Katto to shanpu- onegaishimasu.

perm
パーマ
pa-ma

coloring, dying
カラー
kara-

eyelash extensions
まつエク
matsueku

eyebrow trim
眉カット
mayukatto

hair manicure
ヘアマニキュア
hea manikyua

very short
ベリーショート
beri- sho-to

short
ショート
sho-to

bob cut
ボブ
bobu

undercut
ツーブロック
tsu-burokku

cut in layers
レイヤー
reiya-

shaggy
シャギー
shagi-

Please don't cut my bangs.
前髪は切らないでください。
Maegami wa kiranaide kudasai.

hair on the back of one's head
後ろ髪
ushirogami

straight perm
ストレートパーマ
sutore-to pa-ma

hair straightening
縮毛矯正
shukumo-kyo-se-

hair treatment
トリートメント
tori-tomento

dying gray hair
白髪染め
shiragazome

razor, shaver
顔そり
kaosori

salon offering hair care
ヘッドスパ
heddosupa

hair bleaching
ブリーチ
buri-chi

extensions
エクステ
ekusute

hair dressing
セット
setto

medium-length
ミディアム
midiamu

long
ロング
rongu

Please cut it to about this length.
これくらいにしてください。
kore kurai ni shite kudasai.

sideburns
もみあげ
momiage

hair edges
毛先
kesaki

nape of the neck
えりあし
eriashi

10 Invitations

🔊 051

1 Are you free this weekend?

2 How about we get lunch together?

——Yeah, let's!

——Is next week okay?

3 Sorry. Please invite me again sometime!

4 Want to go somewhere together?

——That sounds great. I'd love to.

5 I'm looking forward to it.

Tips

In Japan, the custom of seniors or men
paying the full bill is not so prevalent.

今週末空いてる?
Konshu-matsu aiteru?

ランチでもどう?
Ranchi demo do-?

――ぜひ!
Zehi!

――来週じゃだめ?
Raishu-ja dame?

残念。また誘って!
Zan'nen. Mata sasotte!

よかったら二人で出かけない?
Yokattara futari de dekakenai?

――うれしい。よろこんで。
Ureshi-. Yorokonde.

楽しみにしてるね!
Tanoshimi ni shiterune!

How about we go for a drive?

よかったらドライブでも。

Yokattara doraibu demo.

lunch
ランチ
ranchi

dinner
ディナー
dina-

sightseeing
観光
kanko-

alcohol
お酒
osake

tea
お茶
ocha

sad
かなしい
kanashi-

get excited
興奮する
ko-funsuru

very satisfied
大満足
daimanzoku

tired
つかれた
tsukareta

disappointed
がっかりした
gakkarishita

surprised
びっくり
bikkuri

Sorry, I'm busy that day.

ごめん、その日は忙しいんだ。

Gomen, sono hi wa isogashi-nda.

have plans
予定がある
yote- ga aru

walk, going on a walk
散歩
sanpo

jogging
ジョギング
jogingu

museum
博物館
hakubutsukan

karaoke
カラオケ
karaoke

bowling
ボーリング
bo-ringu

art museum
美術館
bijutsukan

shopping
買い物
kaimono

zoo
動物園
do-butsuen

aquarium
水族館
suizokukan

happy, fortunate
しあわせ
shiawase

I'm so glad!
うれしい!
Ureshi-!

comfortable
快適
kaiteki

have something one's wants to do
やりたいことがある
yaritai koto ga aru

meet one's family
家族と会う
kazoku to au

work-related
仕事な
shigoto na

 Meeting Up

🔊 053

1 What time is good for you?

——How about 11:30?

2 Is a little later okay?

——Then let's meet at the east gate in Shinjuku at 12:00.

3 Where do you want to have lunch?

4 Why don't you decide?

5 I'll go ahead and make reservations.

6 I'll go ahead and get the tickets.

Tips

Lunchtime in Japan is from around 11:30
to 14:00, and dinner is from around 17:00
to 21:00.

何時頃がいい?
Nanjigoro ga i-?

——11時半は?
Ju-ichiji han wa?

もうちょっと遅くてもいい?
Mo-chotto osokutemo i-?

——じゃあ12時に新宿駅東口で。
Ja- ju-niji ni shinjukueki higashiguchi de.

ランチどこがいいかな?
Ranchi doko ga i-kana?

おまかせしてもいい?
Omakaseshitemo i-?

店は予約しておくね。
Mise wa yoyakushite okune.

チケットとっておくね。
Chiketto totte okune.

A restaurant nearby would be nice.

近い店がいいなぁ。

Chikai mise ga i-na-.

spacious
広い
hiroi

inexpensive, cheap
安い
yasui

famous
有名な
yu-me-na

popular
人気の
ninki no

delicious
おいしい
oishi-

relaxed, calm
落ち着いた
ochitsuita

beautiful
きれいな
kire-na

fashionable
おしゃれな
osharena

casual
カジュアルな
kajuaruna

formal
フォーマルな
fo-maruna

open, vacant
空いている
suiteiru

large amount
量が多い
ryo- ga o-i

lively
にぎやかな
nigiyakana

quiet
静かな
shizukana

Japanese food 和食の *washoku no*	# Do you know the place? 場所わかる? *Basho wakaru?*
Western food 洋食の *yo-shoku no*	# Let's contact each other the day of/on that day. 当日連絡しあおう。 *To-jitsu renraku shiao-.*
Chinese food 中華の *chu-ka no*	# I'm inside the store. 店の中にいるね。 *Mise no naka ni irune.*
Italian food イタリアンの *itarian no*	# Let's meet in front of the building. 建物の前で会おう。 *Tatemono no mae de ao-.*
French フレンチの *furenchi no*	# I'll see you to your house. 家まで迎えに行くよ。 *Ie made mukae ni ikuyo.*
ethnic エスニックの *esunikku no*	# Let's go together from the station. 駅から一緒に行こう。 *Eki kara issho ni iko-.*

Topic

12 Dates

🔊 055

1 Sorry I'm late!

2 Were you waiting for a long time?

3 Would you like a bite?

4 Where should we go?

5 Can I carry your bag for you?

6 I want to go to the Skytree.

7 Here. This is a souvenir for you.

8 I'll go to the station with you.

Tips

While it differs from person to person, most
Japanese are strict about being on time when
meeting up, so it might be best to contact them
if you're going to be more than three minutes late.

遅くなってごめん！
Osokunatte gomen!

待った？
Matta?

ひとくちどう？
Hitokuchi do-?

どこ行こうか？
Doko iko-ka?

荷物持とうか？
Nimotsu moto-ka?

スカイツリーに行ってみたいんだけど。
Sukaitsuri- ni itte mitaindakedo.

これ、おみやげ。どうぞ。
Kore, omiyage. Do-zo.

駅まで送るよ。
Eki made okuruyo.

Hey! This is delicious!

わ!これ、おいしい!

Wa! Kore, oishi-!

sweet
あまい
amai

bitter
にがい
nigai

hot
熱い
atsui

cold
冷たい
tsumetai

thick
厚い
atsui

not delicious
おいしくない
oishikunai

tastes strange
変な味
hen'na aji

greasy, oily
脂っこい
aburakkoi

crispy
しゃきしゃき
shakishaki

crunchy
ぱりぱり
paripari

sticky
ねばねば
nebaneba

dry
ぱさぱさ
pasapasa

chewy
もちもち
mochimochi

crisp
かりかり
karikari

sour すっぱい *suppai*	**spicy** からい *karai*	**salty** しょっぱい *shoppai*
tart しぶい *shibui*	**hard** かたい *katai*	**soft** やわらかい *yawarakai*
thin 薄い *usui*	**smells good** いいにおい *i- nioi*	**juicy** ジューシー *ju-shi-*
flavorless, bland 味がしない *aji ga shinai*	**plentiful** 多い *o-i*	**few** 少ない *sukunai*
crisp and succulent ぷりぷり *puripuri*	**crisp** こりこり *korikori*	**moist** しっとり *shittori*
fluffy, spongy ふわふわ *fuwafuwa*	**smooth** つるつる *tsurutsuru*	**syrupy, slippery** とろとろ *torotoro*

Topic

13 Emergencies

🔊 057

1 Help!

2 Call the police!

3 Fire!

4 Earthquake!

5 Please evacuate!

6 Please stop.

7 I've dropped my wallet.

8 I left my umbrella on the train.

Tips

If you plan on staying for a long period of time,
you should be aware of the evacuation shelters
in your area. You can find them easily on the
Internet by searching for "hinanjo map."

助けてください！
Tasukete kudasai!

警察を呼んでください！
Ke-satsu o yonde kudasai!

火事です！
Kaji desu!

地震です！
Jishin desu!

避難してください！
Hinan shite kudasai!

やめてください。
Yamete kudasai.

財布を落としました。
Saifu o otoshimashita.

電車に傘を忘れました。
Densha ni kasa o wasuremashita.

🔊 058

It's an earthquake! Please evacuate.

地震です！避難してください。

Jishin desu! Hinan shite kudasai.

heavy rain 大雨 *o-ame*
typhoon 台風 *taifu-*

pervert, molester ちかん *chikan*	fight けんか *kenka*	accident じこ *jiko*
water leak みずもれ *mizumore*	gas leak ガスもれ *gasumore*	injury けが *kega*

I left my cell phone on the train.

電車に携帯を忘れました。

Densha ni ke-tai o wasuremashita.

bus バス *basu*
key かぎ *kagi*

flood
洪水
ko-zui

terrorism
テロ
tero

fire
火事
kaji

tsunami
津波
tsunami

strong wind
強風
kyo-fu-

rockfall
がけくずれ
gakekuzure

pickpocket
スリ
suri

Thief! Somebody!
どろぼうです!だれか!
Dorobo- desu! Dareka!

sudden illness
急病
kyu-byo-

room
部屋
heya

store
店
mise

that place from a moment ago
さっきの場所
sakki no basho

glasses
めがね
megane

wallet
さいふ
saifu

book
本
hon

Places and Directions

north
北 kita

west
西 nishi

east
東 higashi

south
南 minami

up
上 ue

inside
中 naka

back
後ろ ushiro

left
左 hidari

right
右 migi

down
下 shita

forward
前 mae

outside
外 soto

Part 4

Sites to See
Must-see Sites
Popular Places

For visitors seeking to enjoy Japan on a deeper level

How to Enjoy ONSEN

1 After paying for admission, men and women enter through separate entrances.

2 You can undress in the changing room and store your clothes in the lockers. Some lockers require that you insert a 100 yen coin, but most return it after use.

3 Grab a towel and head to the bath. If you like, you may bring soap or shampoo with you.

4 Wash your body and hair. Be careful not to splash other people when showering.

5 After rinsing yourself with hot water, carefully and quietly enter the hot spring baths.

6 Gently dry yourself off with your towel, then wring the towel out and return to the changing room.

- Small children can enter the bath with their parents. The age at which young children can enter baths for the opposite sex differs depending on the prefecture. For most places, children up to about 7 years old may enter either bath, but be sure to check with the staff just in case.

6歳 (*rokusai*) 7歳 (*nanasai*) 8歳 (*hassai*)
9歳 (*kyu-sai*) 10歳 (*jussai*)

- Swimsuits are not allowed.
- People with tattoos cannot enter.
- Tie up your hair so it does not fall into the bath water.
- Do not take towels into the bath water. Place them either on your head or in the towel storage area.

- Do not bring smartphones or cameras into the bath house. Please leave them in the changing room.
- Even if the bath is too hot, do not add more water.
- Be sure to dry yourself before entering the sauna.
- Remember to stay hydrated.

Let's go to shrines and temples!

In Japan, regardless of religious beliefs, anyone can visit and worship at any site. Temples are Buddhist institutions and shrines are Shinto institutions. Appearance wise, places that have Buddha statues or graves are temples, and places that have *torii*-style gates are shrines.

At Shrines

1 Bow once at the *torii* gates, like the one in the picture, that are found in front of shrines (this is a way of asking for permission to enter).

2 Just past the gate, you'll find a water basin. Using the spoon-like scoop, pour water over your right hand, then your left hand.

3 Next, hold some water in your left hand and use it to gently rinse your mouth. After that, wash your left once more, since it has touched your mouth.

4 Lastly, wash the scoop's handle for the next person to use as shown in the picture. Then, continue on to the shrine.

5 Once you get to a place that looks like the one in the picture, first, bow slightly. Throw your money into the box, and gently ring the bell if there is one.

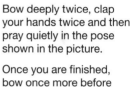

Bow deeply twice, clap your hands twice and then pray quietly in the pose shown in the picture. **6**

Once you are finished, bow once more before you leave.

At Temples

Most of the procedures are the same, but after putting money in the box, you pray by only bowing deeply once without clapping your hands.

Q How much money should you put in the box?

A The word五円(*go'en*) means fate or relationship, and it is also a homonym for the Japanese word for a five-yen coin. For this reason, many people put five-yen coins in the boxes at shrines and temples, but any amount in okay.

Q Why do you wash your hands and mouth?

A The are many theories, such as it is to clean off actual dirt, but most people believe that it is done to wash away evil that can't been seen with the naked eye and to purify the body and the mind before meeting the gods or Buddhist deities.

137

Tokyo

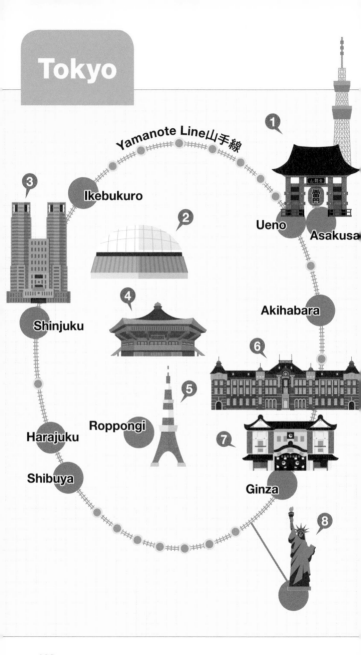

Yamanote Line山手線

1

Ueno

Asakusa

3

Ikebukuro

2

Akihabara

6

Shinjuku

4

Roppongi

5

Harajuku

Shibuya

7

Ginza

8

❶ 雷門 & 東京スカイツリー ®
Kaminari-mon gate & TOKYO SKYTREE®

Asakusa is a popular sightseeing area!
The SKYTREE®, which opened in 2012, is 634 meters high.

❷ 東京ドーム   Tokyo Dome
Live concerts and baseball games are held here.
It even has an amusement park. This is a great place to
spend a whole day.

❸ 東京都庁
**Tokyo Metropolitan Government Office
building**

There are free viewing platforms that give a great view of
Tokyo Tower.

❹ 日本武道館   Nippon Budokan
This is a stadium for kendo, judo and other Japanese
martial arts events.

❺ 東京タワー   Tokyo Tower
This Tokyo landmark stands at 333 meters.
At night, it lights up Tokyo with its warm, candle-like glow.

❻ 東京駅   Tokyo Station
The entrance way to Tokyo, in 2012, construction was
complete on the Maurunouchi side restoring its 100-year-
old red brick design.

❼ 歌舞伎座   Kabukiza
This is a theater dedicated to kabuki, as for of traditional
Japanese theater.

❽ 自由の女神像   Statue of Liberty (Replica)
It stands on the ocean park of Odaiba, a manmade
landmass. Is design is based on the original Statue of
Liberty in New York.

Thank You Messages

Be sure to thank the people that help you out during your stay in Japan!

Your message of thanks will still come across fine in the Roman alphabet.

❶ To. Sayuri
さゆりさんへ
Sayurisan e

❷ Thanks for the wonderful week!
1週間ありがとう!
Isshu-kan arigato-!

❸ I'll be sure to visit Japan again.
ぜったいまた日本に来ます。
Zettai　mata nihon ni kimasu.

Please come visit me in America some time.
さゆりさんも、アメリカにあそびに来てください。
Sayuri-san mo, amerikani asobini kitekudasai.

Sincerely,
お元気で。
Ogenki de.

2017.4.17
Dianna
Dianna より
Dianna yori

❶ When sending a message to someone older or in higher social standing, -sama should be used in place of –sama.

❷ One week can also be replaced with 10 days (10日 <to-ka>), one month (1カ 月 間 <ikkagetsu kan>) or one year (1年間 <ichinen kan>).

Also, for someone older or in higher social standing, arigato-gozaimashita (ありがとうございました) should be used in place of arigato- (ありがとう).

❸ You can also use any of the following phrases

Please do your best with your studies.
▶ 勉強、がんばってね。
Benkyo-, ganbattene.

I'll email you when I get back home.
▶ 帰国したらメールします。
Kikokushitara me-ru shimasu.

Thanks to you, I've learned to love Japan.
▶ さゆりさんのおかげで、日本が大好きになりました。
Sayurisan no okagede, nihon ga daisukini narimashita.

I look forward to the day we meet again.
▶ また会える日を楽しみにしています。
Mata aeruhi o tanoshimini shiteimasu.

Vocabulary list

A		B	
accident	事故 jiko	baby (infant)	赤ちゃん aka chan
address	住所 ju-sho	backpacker	バックパッカー bakkupakka-
admission fee	入場料 nyu-jo-ryo-	bacon	ベーコン be-kon
adult	大人 otona	bag	かばん kaban
age	年齢 nenrei	balance inquiry	残高照会 zandakasho-kai
ahead	先 saki	bar	バー ba-
air conditioner	エアコン eakon	baseball	野球 yakyu-
air mail	航空便 ko-ku-bin	basketball	バスケ basuke
air purifier	空気清浄器 ku-kise-jo-ki	bath	風呂、お風呂 furo, ofuro
airplane	飛行機 hiko-ki	bath robe	部屋着 heyagi
airport	空港 ku-ko-	bath towel	バスタオル basutaoru
alcohol	お酒 osake	beautiful	きれい、きれいな kire-, kire-na
alien (non-Japanese)	外国人 gaikokujin	beef	牛肉 gyu-niku
alien registration	外国人登録 gaikokujin to-roku	beer	ビール bi-ru
always	いつも itsumo	below	下 shita
anemia	貧血 hinketsu	belt	ベルト beruto
animal	動物 do-butsu	bicycle	自転車 jitensha
antiseptic	消毒液 sho-dokueki	bitter	にがい nigai
apartment	アパート apa-to	black tea	紅茶 ko-cha
aquarium	水族館 suizokukan	blanket	毛布 mo-fu
Are you okay?	大丈夫？ daijo-bu?	blend	ブレンド burendo
area	地域 chiiki	book	本 hon
area code	市外局番 shigai kyokuban	botanical garden	植物園 shokubutsu en
arriving at ～	～着 chaku	bottle	びん bin
art museum	美術館 bijutsukan	bound for ～	～行き iki
automobile	自動車 jido-sha	boy	男の子 otoko no ko
awesome/lovely	素敵 suteki	boyfriend	彼氏 kareshi

Braille	点字 tenji
bread	パン pan
bug	虫 mushi
building	建物 tatemono
burn	やけど yakedo
bus	バス basu
bus stop	バス停 basute-
busy	忙しい isogashi-

C

café latte	カフェラテ kaferate
cafeteria	食堂 shokudo-
camera	カメラ kamera
can	かん kan
capital (city)	首都 shuto
car	車 kuruma
car navigation	カーナビ ka- nabi
car number ~	~号車 go-sha
casual	カジュアルな kajuaruna
cat	猫 neko
cell phone	携帯 ke-tai
center	中 naka
central entrance	中央口 chu-o-guchi
change the reservation time	予約時間の変更 yoyaku jikan no henko-
charge (electricity)	充電 ju-den
cheap	安い yasui
check-in	チェックイン chekkuin
check-out	チェックアウト chekkuauto
cheese	チーズ chi-zu
chef	料理人 ryo-rinin
chicken	鶏肉 toriniku

child seat	チャイルドシート chairudo shi-to
Chinese character	漢字 kanji
Chinese food	中華の chu-ka no
chopsticks	はし hashi
Christianity	キリスト教 kirisuto kyo-
city water	水道水 suido- sui
clear weather	晴れ hare
closest	最寄の moyori no
cloudy, cloudiness	くもり kumori
coat	コート ko-to
cockroach	ゴキブリ gokiburi
coffee	コーヒー ko-hi-
cold (food, drink)	冷たい tsumetai
cold (illness)	風邪 kaze
cold (low temperature)	寒い samui
color	色 iro
comfortable	快適 kaiteki
commuter pass	定期券 te-kiken
company worker	会社員 kaishain
computer	パソコン pasokon
conditioner	コンディショナー kondishona-
connecting terminal	連絡口 renrakuguchi
constipation	便秘 benpi
convenience	コンビニ konbini
cooking	料理 ryo-ri
cool (air)	涼しい suzushi-
cool (That's cool!)	かっこいい kakkoi-
corner	角 kado
cough	せき seki
cough drop	のどあめ nodoame

cough lozenge	トローチ toro-chi		draw a map	地図を書いて chizu o kaite
counter	カウンター kaunta-		drive	ドライブ doraibu
coupon ticket	回数券 kaisu-ken		driver's license	運転免許 unten menkyo
crab	かに kani		driver's seat	運転席 unten seki
croissant	クロワッサン kurowassan		dry skin	肌荒れ hadaare
cultural heritage	文化遺産 bunka isan		dryer	ドライヤー doraiya-
culture	文化 bunka		duty-free shop	免税店 menze- ten
cup/glass	コップ／グラス koppu / gurasu		**E**	
cute	かわいい kawai-		earth (planet)	地球 chikyu-
D			earthquake	地震 jishin
day-care center	保育所 hoiku sho		east entrance	東口 higashiguchi
delay	遅延 chien		eating tour	食べ歩き tabearuki
delicious	おいしい oishi-		egg	卵 tamago
departing from ~	～発 hatsu		eight (pieces)	8つ yattsu
deposit	入金 nyu-kin		electric appliance	電化製品 denka se-hin
destination	行先 ikisaki		electric outlet	コンセント konsento
diaper	おむつ omutsu		elementary school student	小学生 sho-gakuse-
diarrhea	下痢 geri		elevator	エレベーター erebe-ta-
dinner	ディナー dina-		embassy	大使館 taishi kan
dirty	汚い kitanai		emergency exit	非常口 hijo- guchi
disabled	障害者 sho-gaisha		entrance	入口 iriguchi
disappointed	がっかりした gakkarishita		escalator	エスカレーター esukare-ta-
discount	割引 waribiki		estimate (prohable cost)	見積り mitsumori
dishwashing soap	食器用洗剤 shokkiyo-senzai		ethnic	エスニックの esunikku no
district	地方 chiho-		euro	ユーロ yu-ro
dizziness	めまい memai		every meal	毎食 maishoku
doctor	先生 sense-		exchange for JPN yen	円に両替 en ni ryo-gae
doctors	医者 isha		exercise	運動 undo-
dollar	ドル doru		exit	出口 deguchi
donuts	ドーナツ do-natsu		expensive	高い takai

express mail	速達 sokutatsu		funny/interesting	おもしろい omoshiroi
express train	急行 kyu-ko-		**G**	
F			game	ゲーム ge-mu
factory outlet	アウトレット auto retto		garbage	ゴミ gomi
fall, autumn	秋 aki		garden	庭 niwa
famous	有名な yu-me-na		girlfriend	彼女 kanojo
(electric) fan	扇風機 senpu-ki		glad	うれしい ureshi-
fare adjustment machine	精算機 se-sanki		glasses	めがね megane
fashionable	おしゃれな osharena		graduate school student	大学院生 daigakuinse-
favorable, going all right	順調 juncho-		greasy, oily	脂っこい aburakkoi
favorite	お気に入り okiniiri		great	すばらしい subarashi-
feeling good	気持ちいい kimochi i-		guitar	ギター gita-
few	少ない sukunai		gum	ガム gamu
fight	けんか kenka		gym	ジム jimu
fire	火事 kaji		**H**	
fire escape	非常階段 hijo- kaidan		ham	ハム hamu
first name	名前 namae		hand towels	おてふき otefuki
first train/bus	始発 shihatsu		hangover	二日酔い futsukayoi
fitting room	試着室 shichaku shitsu		happy, fortunate	しあわせ shiawase
flood	洪水 ko-zui		hard	かたい katai
flour	小麦 komugi		having one's period	生理中 se-richu-
folk	フォーク fo-ku		headache	頭痛 zutsu-
foreign currency	外貨 gaika		health	健康 kenko-
foreigner (non-Japanese)	外国人、外人 gaikoku-jin, gaijin		health food	健康食品 kenko- shokuhin
free (of charge)	無料 muryo-		heartburn	胸焼け muneyake
free, not busy	ひま hima		heater	ストーブ suto-bu
French	フレンチの furenchi no		heating	暖房 danbo-
front	前 mae		heavy rain	大雨 o-ame
front desk	フロント furonto		hiccup	しゃっくり shakkuri
fruit	果物 kudamono		high blood pressure	高血圧 ko-ketsuatsu

145

high humidity	湿度が高い shitsudo ga takai	interpreter	通訳 tsu-yaku
high school stident	高校生 ko-ko-se-	intersection	交差点 ko-saten
highway	高速道路 ko-soku do-ro	invoice	請求書 se-kyu-sho
Hindu	ヒンズー教 hinzu- kyo-	Isram	イスラム教 isuramu kyo-
hockey	ホッケー hokke-	Italian food	イタリアンの itarian no
home	家 ie	itinerary	旅程 ryote-

J

horizontally	横 yoko	jacket	ジャケット jaketto
hose (nylon stocking)	ストッキング sutokkingu	Japanese food	和食の washoku no
hospital	病院 byo-in	Japanese quilted mattress	布団 futon
hot	熱い atsui	Japanese sake	日本酒 nihonshu
hot (coffee)	ホット hotto	Japanese-style room	和室 washitsu
hot (temperature)	暑い atsui	jazz	ジャズ jazu
hot and humid	蒸し暑い mushi atsui	jeans	ジーンズ ji-nzu
hot spring	温泉 onsen	jet lag	時差ボケ jisa boke
hot water	お湯 oyu	job, work	仕事 shigoto
housewife	主婦 shufu	jogging	ジョギング jogingu
husband	旦那さん dannasan	juice	ジュース ju-su

I

		junior high school student	中学生 chu-gakuse-
IC card	ICカード ai shi- ka-do	just right	ちょうどいい cho-do i-
ice	アイス aisu		

K

ice café lattes	アイスカフェラテ aisukaferate	karaoke	カラオケ karaoke
illegal	違法 iho-	kettle	ケトル ketoru
in good spirits, healthy	元気 genki	key	鍵 kagi
inbound	上り nobori	Kids'	キッズ kizzu
inexpensive, cheap	安い yasui	kind (sort, type)	種類 shurui
injury	けが kega	kiosk	キオスク kiosuku
injury, wound	傷 kizu	kitchen	キッチン kitchin
inquiry	問い合わせ toi awase		

L

insured	保険付 hokentsuki		
interpret	通訳して tsu-yakushite	large	大きい o-ki-

146

English	Japanese	Romaji
large amount	量が多い	ryo- ga o-i
laundry detergent	衣料用洗剤	iryo-yo-senzai
left-hand side	左手	hidarite
length	長さ	nagasa
license	免許証	menkyo sho-
life (⇔death)	命	inochi
life (living)	生活	se-katsu
limited express train	特急	tokkyu-
lip balm / cream	リップクリーム	rippu kuri-mu
lipstick	口紅	kuchibeni
lively	にぎやかな	nigiyakana
local express train	準急	junkyu-
local train	各駅停車	kakuekite-sha
locker	ロッカー	rokka-
long	長い	nagai
long hair	ロング	rongu
lost weight, got thin	やせた	yaseta
lotion	化粧水	kesho-sui
low blood pressure	低血圧	te-ketsuatsu
lunch	ランチ	ranchi

English	Japanese	Romaji
mackerel	さば	saba
mailbox	郵便ポスト	yu-bin posuto
making the most of	充実してる	ju-jitsu shiteru
malfunction, breakdown, failure	故障	kosho-
mask	マスク	masuku
massage	マッサージ	massa-ji
matcha latte	抹茶ラテ	matcharate
mature	大人	otona
meal	食事	shokuji

English	Japanese	Romaji
meat	肉類	nikurui
menstrual pain	生理痛	se-ritsu-
Metro station	地下鉄の駅	chikatetsu no eki
microwave	電子レンジ	denshirenji
milk	牛乳	gyu-nyu-
milky lotion	乳液	nyu-eki
moist	しっとり	shittori
moody	気分屋	kibun ya
motion sickness	乗り物酔い	norimonoyoi
movie	映画	e-ga
movie theater	映画館	e-ga kan
mucus, snot	鼻水	hanamizu
museum	博物館	hakubutsukan

English	Japanese	Romaji
nearby	近い	chikai
New Year's Day	正月	sho-gatsu
next to	となり	tonari
nickname	ニックネーム	nikku ne-mu
non-smoking	禁煙	kin'en
north entrance	北口	kitaguchi
not delicious	おいしくない	oishikunai
notebook	ノート	no-to

English	Japanese	Romaji
October	10月	ju-gatsu
Okinawa	沖縄	okinawa
one-way	片道	kata-michi
open, vacant	空いている	suiteiru
opening an account	口座開設	ko-zakaisetsu
operation cancellation	運転見合わせ	untenmiawase
operation suspended	運転中止	untenchu-shi

147

English	Japanese	Romaji
out of service	回送	kaiso-
outbound	下り	kudari
oversleep	寝坊	nebo-

P

English	Japanese	Romaji
pamphlet	パンフ	panfu
pants	ズボン	zubon
parasol	日傘	higasa
partner	パートナー	pa-tona-
payment	支払い	shiharai
peanut	落花生	rakkase-
pedestrian bridge	歩道橋	hodo-kyo-
pedestrian crossing	横断歩道	o-danhodo-
pen	ペン	pen
pencil	鉛筆	enpitsu
pharmacy	薬局	yakkyoku
phone	電話	denwa
pickpocket	スリ	suri
picture	写真	shashin
pill	錠剤	jo-zai
pillow	まくら	makura
plan	計画	ke-kaku
plentiful	多い	o-i
police box	交番	ko-ban
police station	警察署	ke-satsu sho
policeman, policewoman	警察官	ke-satsukan
pollen	花粉	kafun
popular	人気の	ninki no
population	人口	jinko-
pork	豚肉	butaniku
powder medicine	粉薬	konagusuri

English	Japanese	Romaji
power outlet	コンセント	konsento
pregnant	妊娠中	ninshinchu-
prepare	準備する	junbi suru
problem	問題	mondai
public bath	銭湯	sento-
public telephone	公衆電話	ko-shu- denwa

Q

English	Japanese	Romaji
question	質問	shitsumon
quiet	静か、静かな	shizuka, shizukana

R

English	Japanese	Romaji
race (ethnicity)	人種	jinshu
radio	ラジオ	rajio
rain	雨	ame
raincoat	レインコート	reinko-to
rainy season	梅雨	tsuyu
rap	ラップ	rappu
rapid train	快速	kaisoku
raw fish	生魚	namazakana
reading	読書	dokusho
Really?	ほんとに？	honto ni?
rear	一番後ろの	ichiban ushiro no
reason	理由	riyu-
receiving treatment	治療中	chiryo-chu-
reception	受付	uketsuke
recharge	充電	ju-den
refrigerator	冷蔵庫	re-zo-ko
regular train	普通	futsu-
religion	宗教	shu-kyo-
reservation	予約	yoyaku
reserved	予約済み	yoyaku zumi

English	Japanese	Romaji		English	Japanese	Romaji
reserved seat ticket	指定席券	shite-sekiken		shower	シャワー	shawa-
restaurant	レストラン	resutoran		shrimp	えび	ebi
restroom, toilet	トイレ	toire		shrine	神社	jinja
resuming operation	運転再開	untensaikai		sightseeing	観光	kanko-
rich	お金持ち	okanemochi		sightseeing information desk	観光案内所	kanko-an'naijo
right-hand side	右手	migite		sign	看板	kanban
room	部屋	heya		skin	肌	hada
room number	部屋の番号	heya no bango-		skirt	スカート	suka-to
room service	ルームサービス	ru-musa-bisu		sleeper car	寝台車	shindai sha
running out of money	金欠	kinketsu		slippers	スリッパ	surippa

S

English	Japanese	Romaji		English	Japanese	Romaji
				small	小さい	chi-sai
sad	かなしい	kanashi-		smart	頭いい	atamai-
safety box	金庫	kinko		smells good	いいにおい	i- nioi
salad	サラダ	sarada		smoking	喫煙	kitsuen
salmon	さけ	sake		soap	せっけん	sekken
salmon roe	いくら	ikura		socks	くつした	kutsushita
salty	しょっぱい	shoppai		soft	やわらかい	yawarakai
sandwich	サンドイッチ	sandoitchi		sour	すっぱい	suppai
sashimi (thinly-sliced raw fish)	刺身	sashimi		south entrance	南口	minamiguchi
service	サービス	sa-bisu		soy bean	大豆	daizu
sesami seeds	ごま	goma		spacious	広い	hiroi
seven (pieces)	7つ	nanatsu		speaker	スピーカー	supi-ka-
seven people	7人	nananin		spicy	からい	karai
shampoo	シャンプー	shanpu-		spoon	スプーン	supu-n
sheets	シーツ	shi-tsu		sports	スポーツ	supo-tsu
shirt	シャツ	shatsu		spring	春	haru
shochu	焼酎	sho-chu-		stairs	階段	kaidan
shoes	くつ	kutsu		station	駅	eki
shopping	買い物	kaimono		stomachache	腹痛	fukutsu-
short	短い	mijikai		stopping at ～	～方面	ho-men

store	店 mise		television	テレビ terebi
straw	ストロー sutoro-		tennis	テニス tenisu
street tram	路面電車 romen densha		terrorism	テロ tero
strike (stopping of work)	ストライキ sutoraiki		that	それ、あれ sore, are
strong wind	強風 kyo-fu-		thick	厚い atsui
sudden illness	急病 kyu-byo-		thief	どろぼう dorobo-
sugar	さとう sato-		thin	薄い usui
suit	スーツ su-tsu		this	これ kore
suitcase	スーツケース su-tsu ke-su		this address	この住所 kono ju-sho
summer	夏 natsu		this person	この人 konohito
sunblock, sunscreen	日焼けどめ hiyakedome		thunder, lightning	雷 kaminari
sunglass	サングラス san gurasu		ticket counter	きっぷ売り場 kippuuriba
supermarket	スーパー su-pa-		ticket gate	改札 kaisatsu
sweating	汗 ase		ticket machine	券売機 kenbaiki
sweet	あまい amai		tights	タイツ taitsu
swimming	水泳 suie-		tip (gratvity)	チップ chippu
sympathetic	やさしい yasashi-		tired	つかれた tsukareta
T			tool	道具 do-gu
T.V.	テレビ terebi		tooth brush	歯ブラシ haburashi
table	テーブル te-buru		touch	さわる sawaru
tableware	食器 shokki		tour ticket	周遊券 shu-yu-ken
take a break	休む yasumu		towel	タオル taoru
take pictures	写真を撮る shashin o toru		traffic	交通 ko-tsu-
talkative	おしゃべり oshaberi		traffic light	信号 shingo-
tart	しぶい shibui		traffic sign	交通標識 ko-tsu- hyo-shiki
tastes strange	変な味 hen'na aji		train	電車 densha
tax	税金 ze-kin		translation	翻訳 honyaku
taxi	タクシー takushi-		transportation	交通手段 ko-tsu- shudan
tea	お茶 ocha		travel	旅、旅行 tabi, ryoko-
teacher	先生、教師 sense-, kyo-shi		travel agency	旅行代理店 ryoko- dairi ten

English	Japanese	Romaji
travel insurance	旅行保険	ryoko- hoken
trip	旅行	ryoko-
T-shirt	Tシャツ	T shatsu
tsunami	津波	tsunami
two-seater	2人掛けの	futarigake no
typhoon	台風	taifu-

U

umbrella	傘	kasa
underwear	下着	shitagi
uniform	制服	se-fuku
unisex	男女兼用	danjo kenyo-
university student	大学生	daigakuse-

V

vacation	休暇	kyu-ka
vacuum cleaner	掃除機	so-jiki
vehicle number	～両目	ryo-me
vending machine	自販機	jihanki
vertically	縦	tate
very satisfied	大満足	daimanzoku
visit	訪問	ho-mon

W

waiter	ウェイター	uwei ta-
waitress	ウェイトレス	uwei toresu
wake-up call	モーニングコール	mo-ninguko-ru
walk, going on a walk	散歩	sanpo
wallet	さいふ	saifu
warm	暖かい	atatakai
washing machine	洗濯機	sentakuki
watch (wristwatch)	腕時計	ude dokei
water	お水	omizu

English	Japanese	Romaji
water leak	みずもれ	mizumore
weak coffee	アメリカン	amerikan
welcome	歓迎	kange-
west entrance	西口	nishiguchi
Western food	洋食の	yo-shoku no
Western-style room	洋室	yo-shitsu
while eating	食間	shokkan
whiskey	ウィスキー	wisuki-
Why?	なんで？	nande?
wife	奥さん	okusan
wind	風	kaze
window	窓	mado
wine	ワイン	wain
winter	冬	fuyu
withdrawal	引き出し	hikidashi
Women's	レディース	redi-su
wonderful/ amazing	すごい	sugoi
work	仕事	shigoto
world heritage	世界遺産	sekai isan
wrong	間違ってる	machi gatteru

Y

yen	円	en
youth hostel	ユースホステル	yu-su hosuteru

Z

zipe code	郵便番号	yu-bin bango-
zoo	動物園	do-butsuen

Coming to Japan
Simple Japanese Words & Phrases

2017年　3月29日　初版　第1刷発行
2020年　5月15日　　　　第4刷発行

編集・制作	アスク出版編集部
翻訳・翻訳校正	Red Wind
イラスト	秋葉あきこ
カバーデザイン	岡崎裕樹
DTP	朝日メディアインターナショナル
発行人	天谷修身
発行	株式会社アスク出版
	〒162-8558 東京都新宿区下宮比町2-6
	電話03-3267-6864
	https://www.ask-books.com
印刷・製本	大日本印刷株式会社

許可なしに転載、複製することを禁じます。
Printed in Japan
ISBN 978-4-86639-077-2

アンケートにご協力ください

 https://www.ask-books.com/support/

What to Do During an Emergency

◆ **In case of a fire, illness or injury, call an ambulance** ≪ ☎ 119

Available free-of-charge 24 hours a day.
Support available in English.

◆ **In case of an accident or incident, call the police** ≪ ☎ 110

Available free-of-charge 24 hours a day.
Support available in English, and several other languages.

◆ **In case of an earthquake or tremors:**

▸ seek shelter beneath a desk or table.

▸ protect your head with a cushion or book.

▸ stay away from tall furniture.

Once the tremors have subsided:

▸ open the entranceway door to ensure a safe exit.

When evacuating:

▸ turn off your circuit breaker and any gas valves.

▸ write where you are going when leaving your home.

▸ be sure to stay on wide, open roads.

≫ **Emergency phrases on pp. 128–131.**